GETTING STARTED WITH
3D ANIMATION IN UNITY

Animate your 3D Characters in Unity

Patrick Felicia

Getting Started with 3D Animation in Unity

First published: December 2018

Published by Patrick Felicia

CREDITS

Author: Patrick Felicia

BOOKS FROM THE SAME AUTHOR

Unity from Zero to Proficiency (Foundations): In this book, you will become more comfortable with Unity's interface and its core features by creating a project that includes both an indoor and an outdoor environment. This book only covers drag and drop features, so that you are comfortable with Unity's interface before starting to code (in the next book). After completing this book, you will be able to create outdoors environments with terrains and include water, hills, valleys, sky-boxes, use built-in controllers (First- and Third-Person controllers) to walk around the 3D environment and also add and pilot a car and an aircraft.

> Learn more about this book: **https://www.amazon.com/ /dp/B016YF7OKS/**

Unity from Zero to Proficiency (Beginner): In this book, you will get started with coding using C#. The book provides an introduction to coding for those with no previous programming experience, and it explains how to use C# in order to create an interactive environment. Throughout the book, you will be creating a game, and also implementing the core mechanics through scripting. After completing this book, you will be able to write code in C#, understand and apply key programming principles, understand and avoid common coding mistakes, learn and apply best programming practices, and build solid programming skills.

> Learn more about this book: **https://www.amazon.com/dp/B019L2YF4Y/**

Unity from Zero to Proficiency (Intermediate): In this book, you improve your coding skills and learn more programming concepts to add more activity to your game while optimizing your code. The book provides an introduction to coding in C# t. Throughout the book, you will be creating a game, and also implementing the core mechanics through scripting. After completing this book you will be able to write code in C#, understand and apply Object-Oriented Programming techniques in C#, create and use your own classes, use Unity's Finite State Machines, and apply intermediate Artificial Intelligence.

> Learn more about this book: **https://www.amazon.com/dp/B01EJCE85M/**

Unity from Zero to Proficiency (Advanced): In this book, which is the last in the series, you will go from Intermediate to Advanced and get to work on more specific topics to improve your games and their performances. After completing this book, you will be able to create a (networked) multi-player game, access Databases from Unity, understand and apply key design, patterns for game development, use your time more efficiently to create games, structure and manage a Unity project efficiently, optimize game performances, optimize the structure of your game, and create levels procedurally.

> Learn more about this book: **https://www.amazon.com/dp/B01M7PSHUO/**

A Beginner's Guide to 2D Platform Games with Unity: In this book, you will get started with creating a simple 2D platform game. The book provides an introduction to platform games, and it explains how to use C# in order to create an interactive environment.

> Learn more about this book: **https://www.amazon.com/dp/B01MXWPTJ9**

A Beginner's Guide to 2D Shooter Games with Unity: In this book, you will get started with creating a simple 2D shooter game. The book provides an introduction to 2D shooter games, and it explains how to use C# in order to create an interactive environment.

> Learn more about this book: **https://www.amazon.com/dp/B01MYCQ1PM/**

A Beginner's Guide to 2D Puzzle Games with Unity: In this book, you will get started with creating four different types of puzzle games. The book provides an introduction to 2D puzzle games, and it explains how to use C# in order to create four addictive types of puzzle games including: word games (i.e., hangman), memory game (i.e., simon game), card matching game, and a puzzle.

> Learn more about this book: **https://www.amazon.com/dp/B06XQR7SD4**

A Beginner's Guide to Web and Mobile Games with Unity: In this book, you will get started with exporting a simple infinite runner to the web and Android. The book provides an introduction to how to export and share your game with friends on the Web and on Android Play. It provides step-by-step instructions and explains how to easily share a simple game with your friends so that they can play it on your site or an Android device including: processing taps, exporting the game to a web page, debugging your app, signing your app, and much more.

> Learn more about this book: **https://www.amazon.com/dp/B071YXGR1C**

JavaScript from Zero to Proficiency (Beginner): In this book, you will become comfortable with JavaScript using step-by-step and hands-on instructions. This book includes three chapters that painlessly guide you through the necessary skills to code in JavaScript, and implement some very useful features that will add interaction to your page, and improve the user experience. In addition, many of the skills that you will learn in this book will be transferable to other languages.

> Learn more about this book: **https://www.amazon.com//dp/B07FQSH2NX/**

C# from Zero to Proficiency (Beginner): In this book, you will become comfortable with C# using step-by-step and hands-on instructions. With this book, you will not only learn C# but also enjoy the journey, without the frustration. It includes four chapters that painlessly guide you through the necessary skills to code in C#. It assumes no prior knowledge on your part and ensures that you have all the information and explanations that you need every step of the way. All the information is introduced progressively.

> Learn more about this book: **https://www.amazon.com/dp/B07GYN5BV8/**

ABOUT THE AUTHOR

Patrick Felicia is a lecturer and researcher at Waterford Institute of Technology, where he teaches and supervises undergraduate and postgraduate students. He obtained his MSc in Multimedia Technology in 2003 and his PhD in Computer Science in 2009, from University College Cork, Ireland. He has published several books and articles on the use of video games for educational purposes, including the Handbook of Research on Improving Learning and Motivation through Educational Games: Multidisciplinary Approaches (published by IGI), and Digital Games in Schools: a Handbook for Teachers, published by European Schoolnet. Patrick is also the Editor-in-chief of the International Journal of Game-Based Learning (IJGBL), and the Conference Director of the Irish Conference on Game-Based Learning, a popular conference on games and learning organized throughout Ireland.

FREE BOOK & VIDEOS

We all need some extra help and support now and then to keep motivated. So, as you subscribe to my list, you will be able to avail of the following for FREE:

- Access more than 20 video tutorials on Unity for FREE.

- Access an exclusive member area with plenty of resources.

- Receive weekly tips on game design and game programming.

- Gain access to a monthly giveaway where you can win some of my books on Unity and video courses for FREE.

- Get notified and receive my books weeks before they are published.

- Join a community of over 2000 subscribers and Unity fans who can help you when you need it.

- You can, of course, unsubscribe at any time, if you don't want to receive helpful and quality content anymore.

You can subscribe using this link (http://learntocreategames.com/subscribe/) or by pressing the next button.

SUBSCRIBE

SUPPORT AND RESOURCES FOR THIS BOOK

To complete the different activities included in this book, you will need to download the resource pack for this book; it includes animated 3D models, textures, and C# scripts for some of the sections in this book. To download these resources, please do the following.

If you are already a member of my list, you can just go to the member area (**http://learntocreategames.com/member-area/**) using the usual password and you will gain access to all the resources for this book.

If you are not yet on my list, you can do the following:

- Open the following link: **http://learntocreategames.com/books/**

- Select this book ("**Getting Started with 3D Animation in Unity**").

- On the new page, click on the link labelled "**Book Files**", or scroll down to the bottom of the page.

- In the section called "**Download your Free Resource Pack**", enter your email address and your first name, and click on the button labeled "**Yes, I want to receive my bonus pack**".

- After a few seconds, you should receive a link to your free start-up pack.

- When you receive the link, you can download all the resources to your computer.

This book is dedicated to Mathis & Helena

TABLE OF CONTENTS

PREFACE

After teaching Unity for over 5 years, I always thought it could be great to find a book that could get my students started with Unity in a few hours and that showed them how to master the core functionalities offered by this fantastic software.

Many of the books that I found were too short and did not provide enough details on the reasons behind the actions recommended and taken; other books were highly theoretical, and I found that they lacked practicality and that they would not get my students' full attention. In addition, I often found that game development may be preferred by those with a programming background, but that people with an Arts background, even if they wanted to know how to create games, often had to face the challenge of learning to code for the first time.

As a result, I started to consider a format that would cover both aspects: be approachable (even to the students with no programming background), keep students highly motivated and involved, using an interesting project, cover the core functionalities available in Unity to get started with game programming, provide answers to common questions, and also provide, if need be, a considerable amount of details for some topics.

I then created a book series entitled **Unity from Zero to Proficiency** that did just that. It gave readers the opportunity to discover Unity's core features, especially those that would make it possible to create an interesting 3D game rapidly. After reading this book series, many readers emailed me to let me know how the book series helped them; however, they also mentioned that they wanted to be able to delve into specific features in more details.

This is the reason why I created this new book series entitled **Getting Started with**; it is for people who would like to focus on and get started with a specific aspect of their game development with Unity.

In this book, focused on 3D Character Animation in Unity, you will learn how to master all the features available in Unity to animate your 3D characters.

After completing this book, you will be able to:

- Quickly attach animations to an existing 3D character.

- Import a 3D Character in Unity.

- Create a 3rd Person-controller from an imported character (i.e., moving, managing interactions and collisions).

- Make a character walk, run, or jump in Unity.

- Apply animations to 3D characters.

- Use a finite-state machine to determine the character's movements and animations.

- Use transitions, sub-state machines and parameters in Unity (i.e., Mecanim).

- Blend animations.

- Use the same behaviour for different characters.

- Use blend trees in Unity to achieve smooth transitions between animations.

- Control animations from your script.

CONTENT COVERED BY THIS BOOK

- Chapter 1, *Creating Your Character*, explains how you can create, animate and import your 3D character so that it can be used in Unity.

- Chapter *Using Finite State Machines*, provides step-by-step instructions so that you can start to control your 3D character through a Finite-State Machine and C#. You will learn how to create states with their corresponding animations, and how to transition between states using parameters and by controlling these from a C# script.

- Chapter 3, *Using 1-Dimensional Blend Trees*, provides an introduction to blend trees, whereby you can blend animations based on a single parameter to make these transitions smoother.

- Chapter 4, *Using 2D Blend Trees*, further explains and illustrates the concept of blend trees but this time with two parameters. Using this chapter, you will be able to smoothly switch between animations for your 3D character, based on its speed and direction.

- Chapter 5, *Polishing-Up the Character and Adding Animations*, explains how you can fix common issues linked to importing 3D character, and it also shows you how to make your character jump, or how to reuse the same animator controller for different character, and save you a lot of time in the process.

- Chapter 6 provides answers to Frequently Asked Questions (FAQs) related to the topics covered in this book.

- Chapter 7 summarizes the topics covered in this book and provides you with more information on the next steps to follow.

WHAT YOU NEED TO USE THIS BOOK

To complete the project presented in this book, you only need Unity 2018 (or a more recent version) and to also ensure that your computer and its operating system comply with Unity's requirements. Unity can be downloaded from the official website (**http://www.unity3d.com/download**), and before downloading it, you can check that your computer is up to scratch on the following page: **http://www.unity3d.com/unity/system-requirements**. At the time of writing this book, the following operating systems are supported by Unity for development: Windows XP (i.e., SP2+, 7 SP1+), Windows 8, and Mac OS X 10.6+. In terms of graphics card, most cards produced after 2004 should be suitable.

In terms of computer skills, all knowledge introduced in this book will assume no prior programming experience from the reader. So for now, you only need to be able to perform common computer tasks, such as downloading items, opening and saving files, be comfortable with dragging and dropping items and typing, and be relatively comfortable with Unity's interface.

So, if you would prefer to become more comfortable with Unity prior to starting this book, you can download the books in the series called Unity From Zero to Proficiency (Foundations, Beginner, or Intermediate, Advanced). These books cover most of the shortcuts and views available in Unity, as well as how to perform common tasks in Unity, such as creating and transforming objects, importing assets, using navigation controllers, creating scripts or exporting the game for the web.

WHO THIS BOOK IS FOR

If you can answer **yes** to all these questions, then this book is for you:

1. Would you like to learn how to animate your 3D characters in Unity?

2. Would you like to know how to control your 3D characters and feature smooth animations?

3. Would you like to learn more about Mecanim and blend trees?

4. Although you may have had some prior exposure to Unity and coding, would you like to delve more into 3D Character Animation?

WHO THIS BOOK IS NOT FOR

If you can answer yes to all these questions, then this book is **not** for you:

1. Can you already create and animate your 3D characters in Unity?

2. Are you looking for a reference book on 3D Character Animation?

3. Are you a professional Unity developer?

If you can answer yes to all four questions, you may instead look for the other books in the series on the official website (**http://www.learntocreategames.com**).

HOW YOU WILL LEARN FROM THIS BOOK

Because all students learn differently and have different expectations of a course, this book is designed to ensure that all readers find a learning mode that suits them. Therefore, it includes the following:

- A list of the learning objectives at the start of each chapter so that readers have a snapshot of the skills that will be covered.

- Each section includes an overview of the activities covered.

- Many of the activities are step-by-step, and learners are also given the opportunity to engage in deeper learning and problem-solving skills through the challenges offered at the end of each chapter.

- Each chapter ends-up with a quiz and challenges through which you can put your skills (and knowledge acquired) to the test. Challenges consist in coding, debugging, or creating new features based on the knowledge that you have acquired in the chapter.

- The book focuses on the core skills that you need. While some sections go into more detail, once concepts have been explained, links are provided to additional resources, where necessary.

- The code is introduced progressively and it is also explained in detail.

- You also gain access to several videos that help you along the way, especially for the most challenging topics.

FORMAT OF EACH CHAPTER AND WRITING CONVENTIONS

Throughout this book, and to make reading and learning easier, text formatting and icons will be used to highlight parts of the information provided and to make the book easy to read.

SPECIAL NOTES

Each chapter includes resource sections, so that you can further your understanding and mastery of Unity; these include:

- A quiz for each chapter: these quizzes usually include 10 questions that test your knowledge of the topics covered throughout the chapter. The solutions are provided on the companion website.

- A checklist: it consists of between 5 and 10 key concepts and skills that you need to be comfortable with before progressing to the next chapter.

- Challenges: each chapter includes a challenge section where you are asked to combine your skills to solve a particular problem.

Author's notes appear as described below:

| Author's suggestions appear in this box. |

Code appears as described below:

```
public int score;
public string playersName = "Sam";
```

Checklists that include the important points covered in the chapter appear as described below:

- Item1 for check list.

- Item2 for check list.

- Item3 for check list.

HOW CAN YOU LEARN BEST FROM THIS BOOK?

- **Talk to your friends about what you are doing.**

  We often think that we understand a topic until we have to explain it to friends and answer their questions. By explaining your different projects, what you just learned will become clearer to you.

- **Do the exercises.**

  All chapters include exercises that will help you to learn by doing. In other words, by completing these exercises, you will be able to better understand the topics and gain practical skills (i.e., rather than just reading).

- **Don't be afraid of making mistakes.**

  I usually tell my students that making mistakes is part of the learning process; the more mistakes you make and the more opportunities you have for learning. At the start, you may find the errors disconcerting, or you may find that Unity does not work as expected until you understand what went wrong.

- **Challenge yourself.**

  All chapters include a challenge section where you can decide to take on a particular challenge to improve your game or skills. These challenges are there for you to think creatively and to apply the knowledge that you have acquired in each chapter using a problem-based approach.

- **Learn in chunks.**

  It may be disconcerting to go through five or six chapters straight, as it may lower your motivation. Instead, give yourself enough time to learn, go at your own pace, and learn in small units (e.g., between 15 and 20 minutes per day). This will do at least two things for you: it will give your brain the time to "digest" the information that you have just learned, so that you can start fresh the following day. It will also make sure that you don't "burn-out" and that you keep your motivation levels high.

FEEDBACK

While I have done everything possible to produce a book of high quality and value, I always appreciate feedback from readers so that the book can be improved accordingly. If you would like to give feedback on this book, you can email me at **learntocreategames@gmail.com**.

IMPROVING THE BOOK

Although great care was taken in checking the content of this book, I am human, and some errors could remain in the book. As a result, it would be great if you could let me know of any issue or error you may have come across in this book, so that it can be solved and so that the book can be updated accordingly. To report an error, you can email me (learntocreategames@gmail.com) with the following information:

- Name of the book.

- The page or section where the error was detected.

- Describe the error and also what you think the correction should be.

Once your email is received, the error will be checked, and, in the case of a valid error, it will be corrected, and the book will be updated to reflect the changes accordingly.

SUPPORTING THE AUTHOR

A lot of work has gone into this book and it is the fruit of long hours of preparation, brainstorming, and finally writing. As a result, I would ask that you do not distribute any illegal copies of this book.

This means that if a friend wants a copy of this book, s/he will have to buy it through the official channels (i.e., through Amazon or the book's official website: **http://www.learntocreategames.com/books)**.

If some of your friends are interested in the book, you can refer them to the book's official website **(http://www.learntocreategames.com/books)** where they can either buy the book, or join the mailing list to be notified of future promotional offers or enter a monthly draw and be in for a chance to receive a free copy of the book.

1
CREATING YOUR CHARACTER

In this section, we will go through some very simple steps to create the character that you will be using in Unity, including:

- Using Mixamo, a free online software, to select a character for your game.

- Animating your character in Mixamo.

- Exporting your animated character so that it can be used in Unity.

So, after completing this chapter, you will be able to:

- Select your own 3D character.

- Select and apply different types of animations to your character.

- Export your character and the associated animations so these can be used in Unity for your game.

The necessary resources and code solutions for this chapter are included in the **resource pack** that you can download by following the instructions included in the section entitled **"Support and Resources for this Book"**.

CREATING YOUR CHARACTER

For this part of the book, we will have a look at Mixamo which is an online software that makes it possible to create and animate 3D characters. The idea, when using this software is to create and animate your characters, and then to import them so that they can be used in Unity.

> If for some reason, you would prefer not to use Mixamo, the animated characters used in this chapter are available in your resource pack that you can download by following the instructions included in the section entitled "**Support and Resources for this Book**".

- Please open the following page in your browser: **http://mixamo.com**.

- Once the page is open, you can click on the button labelled **Login**, if you already have an account for this site.

- You can also click on the button **Sign-up for FREE**, to create an account otherwise.

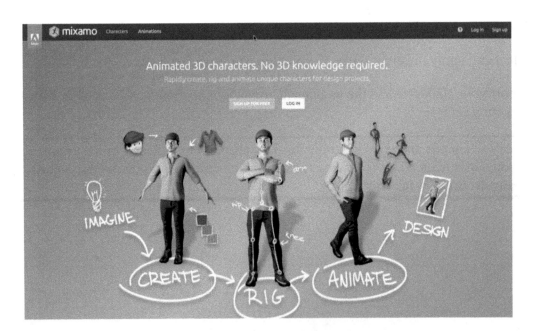

Figure 1-1: Opening the site mixamo.com

- If you chose to create an account, the following window should appear:

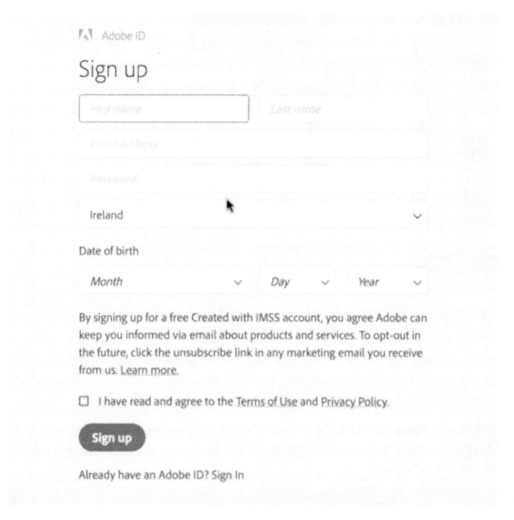

Figure 1-2: Signing-up to Mixamo

After signing-up, and completing all the necessary steps, you should now be able to login.

- As soon as you are logged-in, you will have the choice to select your own character and animation.

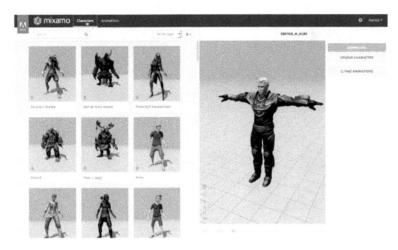

Figure 1-3: Starting Mixamo

- To start with, we will select a new character; to do so, please press the tab called **Character** located in the top-left part of the window.

- Once this is done, a list of characters that you can use for your games will be displayed; these characters are already textured and rigged which means that they include a skeleton that makes it possible for them to be animated later.

For this example, but again you can choose any character if you wish, we will select the character **dreyar**, by clicking on the corresponding image on the left hand side of the screen, as per the next figure.

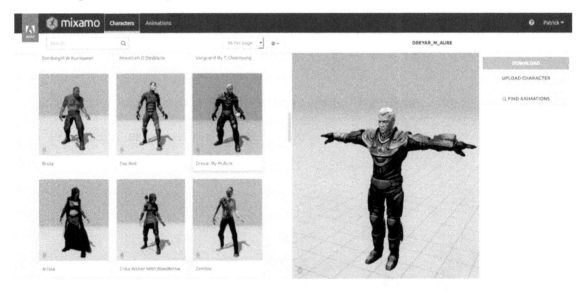

Figure 1-4: Selecting your character

- If a window asking you to "**go ahead although the previous character will not be saved**" appears, please press the button labelled "**Use this character**", as per the next figure

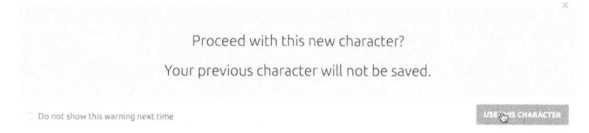

Proceed with this new character?

Your previous character will not be saved.

Do not show this warning next time

USE THIS CHARACTER

Figure 1-5: Confirming your character selection

Once this is done, you will be able to see the character that you have selected in the right-hand side of the screen, in what is often called a **T pose** (often called the reference pose), as per the next figure, which means that the character is not yet animated.

Figure 1-6: The character in the T pose

ANIMATING YOUR CHARACTER

So at this stage you have selected a character, and the next step is to be able to add some animations to the character.

- Please click on the tab called **Animation**, located in the top-left corner of the window.

- You should now see a list of animations made available to you by Mixamo.

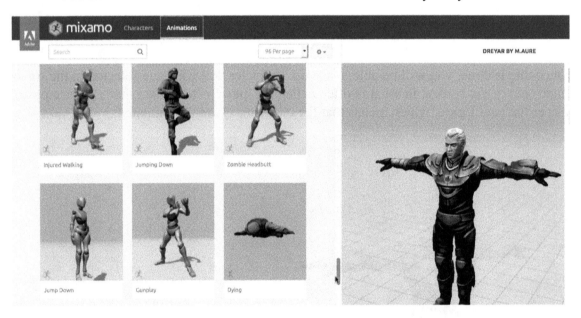

Figure 1-7: Selecting animations

Note that the character that you see on the animation is not the final animated character, but just a representation of how the animation that you are about to apply to your character would look like.

To look for specific types of animation, you can use the menu located in the top-left corner of the window, as per the next figure.

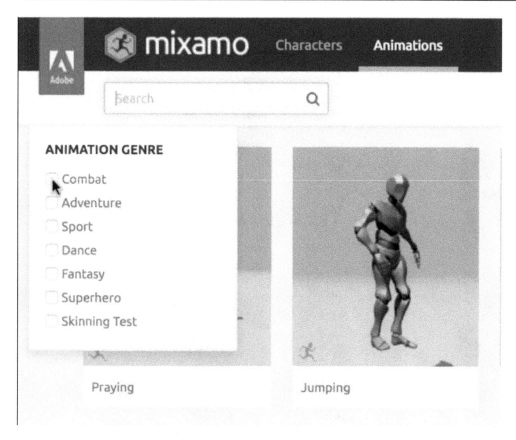

Figure 1-8: Filtering through the animations

This menu makes it possible to filter through the animations by genre (e.g., Combat, Adventure, Sport, etc.)

You can also, if need be, perform a search, by using the search window available in the top left corner of the window. In our case, because we will be looking for a walking animation, we can type the text **walking** in the search field.

Figure 1-9: Searching for an animation

After pressing **Enter** on your keyboard, Maximo will display a list of animations for which the name includes the word **walking**.

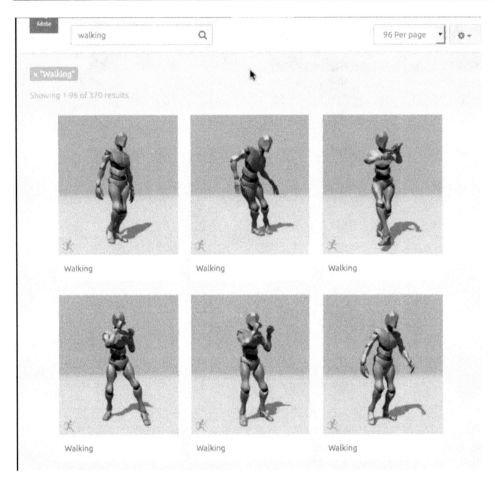

Figure 1-10: Displaying the results of the search

In our case, we will select the very first **animation** called **walking** (the first animation in the top left corner), by clicking on this animation.

After a few seconds, you should see that you character located in the right part of the window is animated, using the animation that you have just picked as per the next figure.

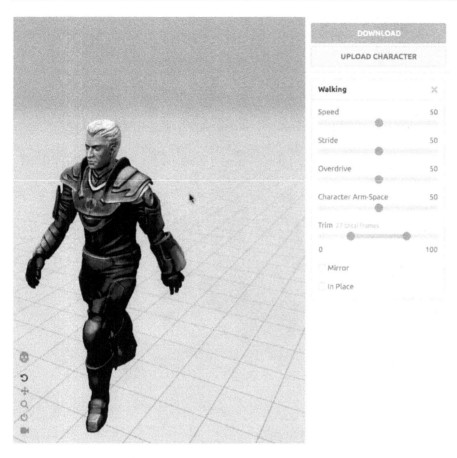

Figure 1-11: Applying an animation to our character

As you will see, the character is animated, however, it doesn't stay on the spot, and it is difficult to see the full animation. To remedy this problem, you can tick the box for the option called "**In place**", located in the right part of the window.

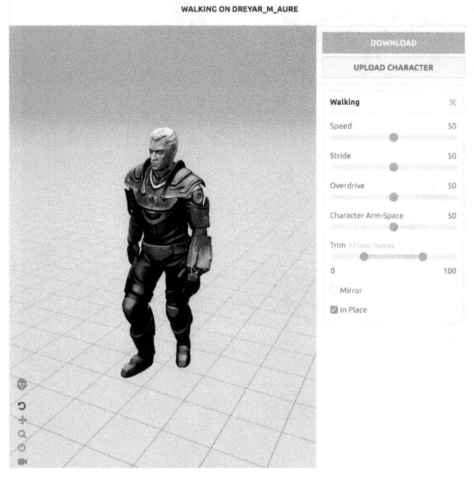

WALKING ON DREYAR_M_AURE

Figure 1-12: Using the "In Place" option

In fact, for your game, you only need this animated character to walk on the spot, as the overall movement (i.e., going left, right, forward and back) will be managed through Unity. Also note that you can modify some of the other parameters if you wish (e.g., speed, overdrive, etc.)

Once this animation has been applied, we can now save it.

- Please lick on the button labelled **Download**.

- In the new window, select the format FBX for Unity (**.fbx**) and leave all the other options as default, and then click on the button **Download**.

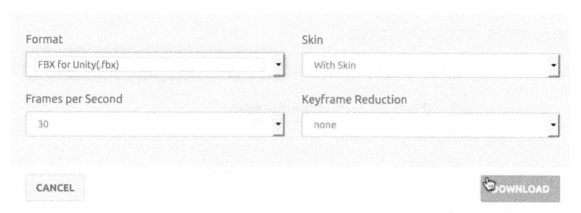

Figure 1-13: Setting the download options

- The browser will ask you where you would like to download this file (**dreyar_m_aure@Walking.fbx**).

- Please save the file to a location of your choice.

IMPORTING YOUR CHARACTER

So at this stage you have saved your animation, and we will now import it in Unity.

- Please open Unity, if this is not already done.

- Create a new project in Unity.

- In the new scene, please make sure that the **Project** window is visible.

- Return to your file system where the animation was saved. In my case, the animation was called **dreyar_m_aure@walking.fbx**.

- Drag and drop the file **dreyar_m_aure@walking.fbx** from your file system to the **Project** window in Unity, as illustrated in the next figure.

Figure 1-14: Importing the animation

Once this is done, this should create a file called **dreyar aure@walking.fbx**, a folder called **dreyar_m_aure@walking.fbm**, along with another folder called **Materials** in the **Project** window.

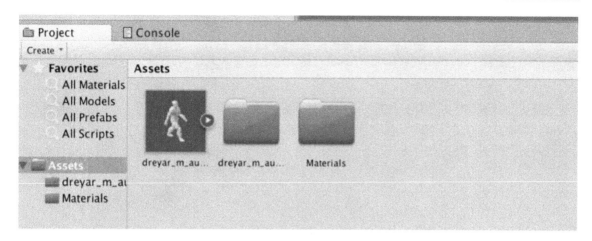

Figure 1-15: The folders created after the import

Now that we have imported our character and its dependencies, we can start to create a ground on which this character will walk.

- Please create a new box: select **GameObject | 3D Object | Cube**.

- Set its **x** and **z** scale attributes to **100**.

Next, we will create another cube that will be used to assess (and to subsequently readjust) the size of our character. This is because the scale factor used when creating this object might not match our project.

- Please create a new cube: select **GameObject | 3D Object | Cube**.

- You can then move this cube just above the ground. By default, this cube will be 1 meter wide.

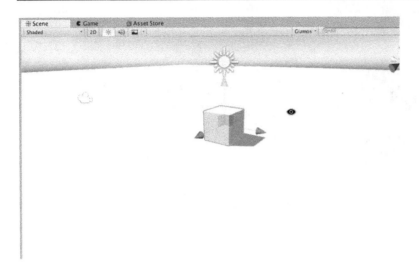

Figure 1-16: Adding a cube to gauge the size of the 3D model

Once this is done, we can add our imported 3D character to the scene near the cube, to check if its original scaling is correct.

- Please drag and drop the object **dreyar_m_aure@walking.fbx** from the **Project** window to the **Scene** view.

As you will probably see, this character, when added to the scene, is approximately 10 times bigger that the small box; this means that we will need to rescale the character accordingly and divide its size by 10 (or multiply by .01).

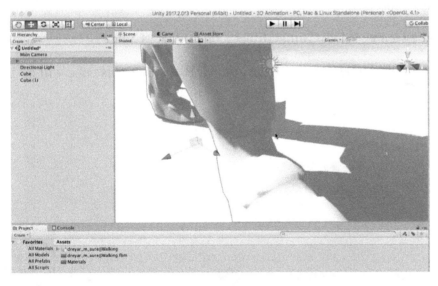

Figure 1-17: Adding the character to the scene

So let's proceed with the rescaling:

- Please click once on the object called **dreyar_m_aure.fbx** from the **Project** window.

- Check that the **Inspector** window is open.

- In the **Inspector** window, click on the tab called **Model**.

- In this tab, enter the value **0.1** for the attribute called **scale** and then press on the button labeled **Apply** located in the bottom-right corner of the **Inspector** window, as per the next figure.

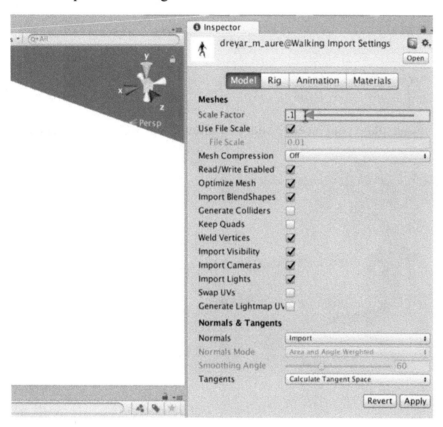

Figure 1-18: Rescaling the character

After clicking on the **Apply** button, you should see that the character has been rescaled, and that its size is now more realistic (about 1.8 m), as per the next figure.

Figure 1-19: The character after changing the scale

Once this is done, you can play your scene, and you should see that the character is immobile.

Figure 1-20: The character is immobile

The reason for the absence of animation is that this character in order to be animated, needs to be added a component that is called an **Animator Controller**; this component will be in charge of deciding what animation should be played for a specific 3D character and when.

- First, please click on the object called **dreyar_m_aure@walking** in the **Hierarchy** window.

- We could rename it **NPC**, for now.

- Then look at the **Inspector** window.

- You should see that this object has a component called **Animator**; however, its attribute called **Controller** is empty, as illustrated in the next figure.

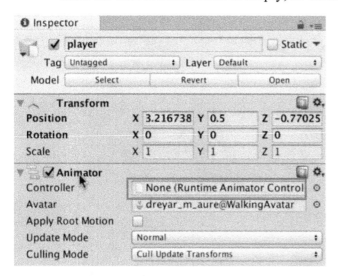

Figure 1-21: Displaying the Animator Component

So, we need an **Animator Controller** to be able to animate our character and we will create one accordingly.

- In the **Project** window, select: **Create | Animator Controller**.

- A new **Animator Controller** will be created; you can rename it **ControlNPC**, for example.

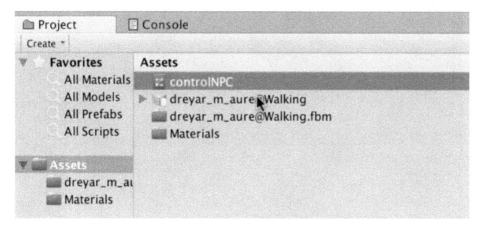

Figure 1-22: Renaming the Animator Controller

Once this is done, we can apply this **Animator Controller** to our 3D character:

- Please select the object **NPC** in the **Hierarchy**.

- Drag and drop the **Animator Controller** called **controlNPC** from the **Project** window to the attribute **Controller** for the component **Animator**, as per the next figure.

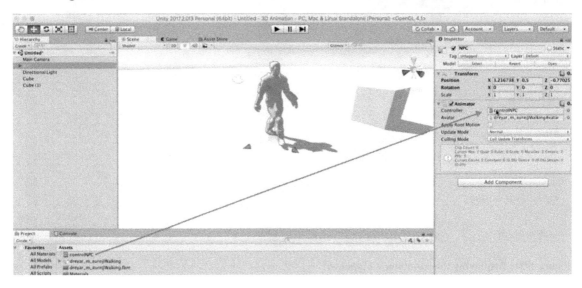

Figure 1-23: Applying the new controller to the 3D Character

Once this **Animator Controller** has been created and linked to our character, we need to set it up, so that we can specify that the walking animation should be used for this character.

- Please double click on the **Animator Controller** called **ControlNPC** in the **Project** window.

- This will open the **Animator** window, as per the next figure.

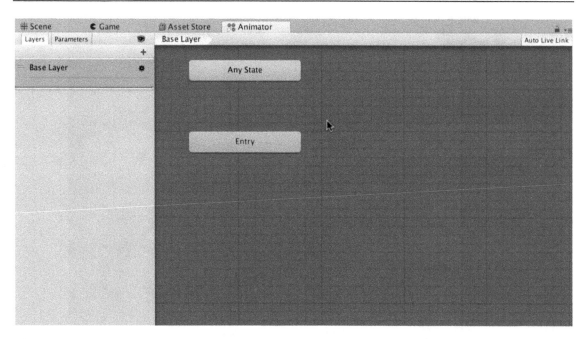

Figure 1-24: Opening the Animator window

The animator window helps to manage what is often called a **Finite State Machine**. Put simply, this means that the software, or the game for our purpose, will include several states, but will be in one state and one state only at any given time.

For our purpose, we need to specify the initial state for our character, and the type of animation that will be played in this particular state.

- Please right-click on the canvas, and then select: **Create State | Empty** from the contextual menu.

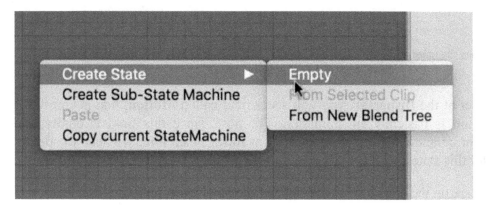

Figure 1-25: Creating a new state

This will create an empty state, as per the next figure.

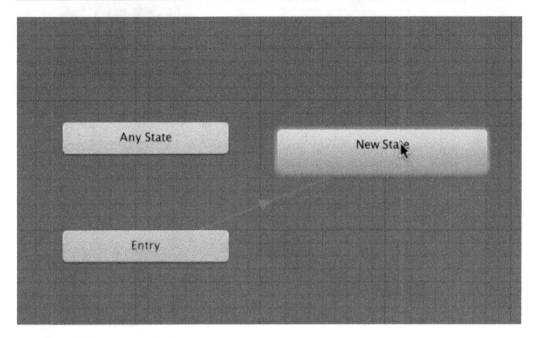

Figure 1-26: The new state has been created

As per the previous figure, you will see an arrow pointing from the state **Entry** to the state called **New State**. This means that whenever the game starts (the point of "**Entry**"), the default and active state will be **New State**.

- So we could rename this state: please select the state called **New Sate**, and using the **Inspector**, change its name to **walking**.

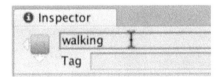

Figure 1-27: Changing the name of the state

If you look closer at the **Inspector**, you will see a field called **Motion**, that is empty for now. So a motion is basically an animation. For now, since this field is empty, the character will not be animated in the state called **walking**; therefore, we need to specify an animation for this state.

- Please click on the cogwheel to the right of the label **Motion** in the Inspector.

- This will open a new window called "**Select Motion**".

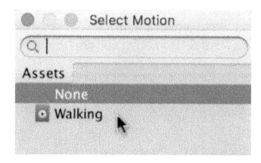

Figure 1-28: Selecting an animation

- In the search window, the only animation available is called **Walking**; it was imported with the animated character created in Maximo.

- You can double click on this animation to select it.

- You should now see that the state **walking** has the associated **Motion** (or animation) called **Waking**, as per the next figure.

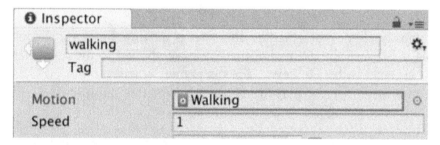

Figure 1-29: Adding an animation

By the way, you can check the animation that you have imported from Maximo by expanding the object **dreaymar_m_aure.fbx** in the **Project** window, as per the next figure.

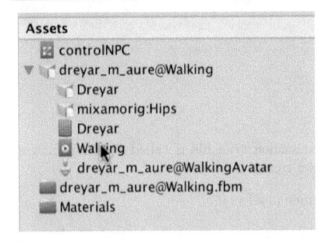

Figure 1-30: Displaying the embedded animations

If you play your scene, you should now see that the character is moving, but that its stops after a few seconds; this is because the animation that we have applied to the character was not set-up to loop automatically. However, for our game, whenever the NPC is walking, we want his/her animation to be played indefinitely. For this purpose, we will need to modify the attributes of the animation. So let's proceed:

- Please rearrange the layout of the window so that the **Animator** window is displayed besides the **Console** window, as per the next figure.

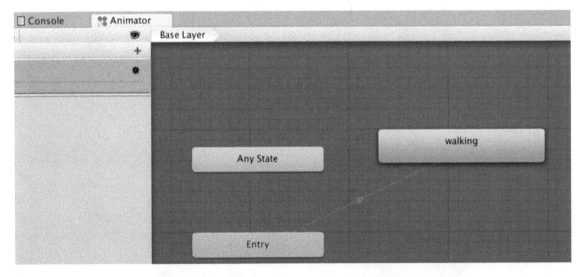

Figure 1-31: Modifying the layout

- Next, double-click on the state called **walking**, so that the properties of the animation linked to this state can be displayed in the **Inspector** window.

- Once this is done, in the **Inspector** window, scroll down to the section called **Loop Time**, and set the attribute **Loop Time** to **true** by clicking on the corresponding tick box, as specified in the next figure.

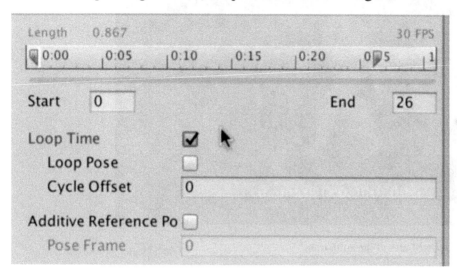

Figure 1-32: Looping the animation

Once this is done, and to check that the animation will play properly, you can press the play button, that is within the **Inspector** window (i.e., at the bottom of the window), and it should display the animated character walking on the spot indefinitely.

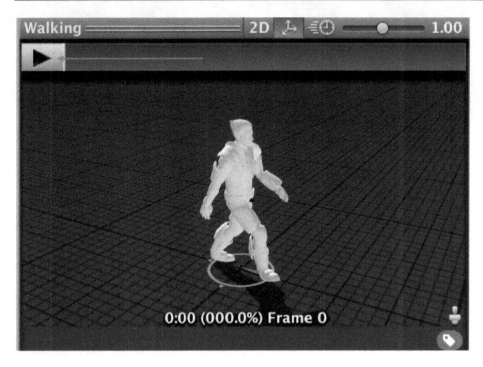

Figure 1-33: Checking the attributes of the animation

- Once you are happy with this change, you can press the button labeled **Apply**, located in the bottom-right corner of the **Inspector**.

- You can now play the scene again, and you should see that the character is now walking indefinitely.

You may notice, in the **Animator** window, a blue progression bar for the state called **walking**, as per the next figure.

Figure 1-34: Displaying the active state

This bar indicates that we are currently in the state called **walking**.

The only issue at this stage is that, while we can see and focus on our character properly using the **Scene** view, it may not appear fully in the game view; so we just need to ensure that the current camera is following our character. To do so, we will import a different type of camera that has the ability to follow a specific target. This camera is included in a package that we need to import. So let's import and use this camera:

- Please select **Assets | Import Package | Cameras**.

- A new window will appear.

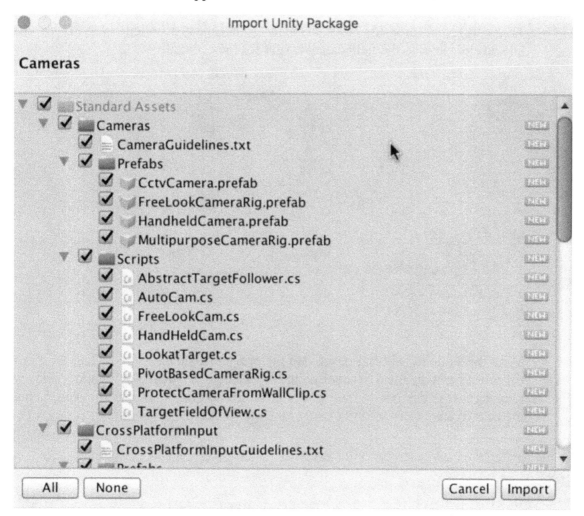

Figure 1-35: Importing the package Cameras

- You can press the button labelled **Import**.

- This will create a folder called **Cameras** within the folder **Standard Assets**.

- Using the **Project** window, please navigate to the folder **Assets | Standard Assets | Camera | Prefabs**.

- Drag and drop the prefab called **MultipurposeCameraRig** to the **Scene** view.

- This will create a new object in the **Hierarchy** called **MultipurposeCameraRig**. As mentioned earlier, this camera is designed to follow a specific target, so we need to specify this target as the 3D character, so that the camera can follow our character.

- Please select the object **MultipurposeCameraRig** in the **Hierarchy**.

- Then drag and drop the 3D character (the object labelled as **NPC** in the **Hierarchy** view) to the field called **target** for the camera.

Figure 1-36: Setting the target for the camera

- Once this is done, you can deactivate the previous camera named **Main Camera** by selecting it in the **Hierarchy**, and by using the **Inspector** window and by clicking on the tick box to the right of its name, so that the box is unticked, as per the next figure.

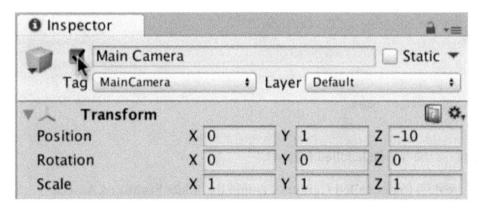

Figure 1-37: Deactivating the main camera

You can now play the scene and you should see that the new camera is now following the main character.

LEVEL ROUNDUP

In this chapter, we have managed to import an animated character in Unity and to also use a Finite-State Machine so that the animation is applied to our character in Unity. We have also added a camera that follows the character.

Checklist

 You can consider moving to the next stage if you can do the following:

- Import a 3D character in Unity.

- Create an Animation Controller.

- Create a State.

- Apply an animation to a specific state.

Quiz

Now, let's check your knowledge! Please answer the following questions or specify whether these statements are either correct or incorrect (the solutions are on the next page).

1. A **Finite-Sate Machine** is used in Unity for character animation.

2. The attribute **Loop Pose** can be used to ensure that an animation is looping.

3. An **Animator Controller** includes the state **Entry** by default.

4. For a character to be animated in Unity, its current state needs to be associated to an animation.

5. It is not possible to rescale a 3D character in Unity.

6. It is possible to preview the changes made to an animation in Unity before applying these changes.

7. States can be created using the window called **Animation**.

8. By default, a state has an associated animation.

9. An **Animator Controller** needs to be added to an **Animator**, so that a 3D character can be animated.

10. It is possible to change the name of a state after it has been created.

Solutions to the Quiz

1. True.

2. True.

3. True.

4. True.

5. False.

6. True.

7. False (it is the **Animator** window).

8. False.

9. True.

10. True.

2

USING FINITE STATE MACHINES

In this section, we will start to work more with Finite-State Machines in Unity. We will create new animations and apply them to the character that will be controlled by the player. Some of the objectives of this section will be to:

- Show how to link states.

- Show how to create transitions between states.

- Illustrate how to trigger transitions using the Animator window.

- Illustrate how to trigger transitions using C#.

After completing this chapter, you will be able to:

- Create additional animations for your character.

- Associate new states with these animations.

- Create and control transitions between these states.

- Control your NPC using the keyboard.

- Write the code to ensure that the animations are played based on the current state.

CONTROLLING YOUR CHARACTER

The idea here is to create a second animation for when the character is idle. This will be the default state for the character, until the player presses a key on the keyboard, which should cause the character to move accordingly. So let's create this idle animation.

If you prefer not to use Mixamo to create the animations, these animations are also available in the resource pack that you can download by following the instructions included in the section entitled "**Support and Resources for this Book**".

- Please open the page for Mixamo: **http://www.mixamo.com**.

- Once you are logged-in, please select the tab called **Animations**.

- Using the search field, look for the animations that include the word **idle**.

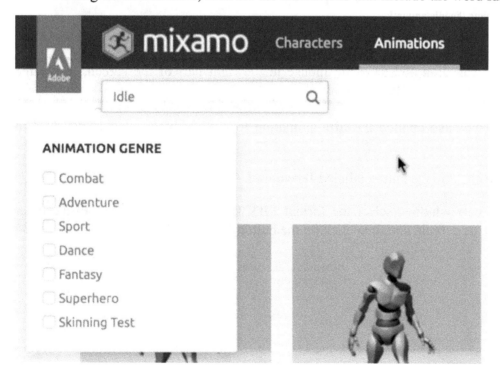

Figure 2-1: Searching for idle animations

- Once the results are displayed, you can select the **idle** animation of your choice; in my case, I selected the first one in the list.

- Once this is done, the character on the right should be displayed with an **idle** animation.

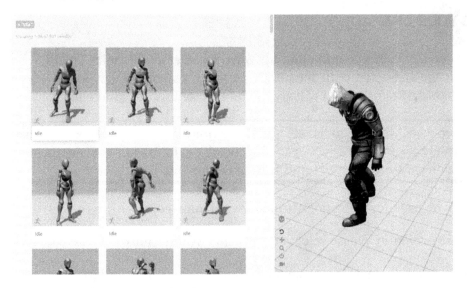

Figure 2-2: Applying the idle animation

Note that you can drag and drop the mouse in the right part of the screen, to see the animated character from different angles.

At this stage we have applied the **idle** animation to our character; so we just need to download it.

- Please click on the button labeled **Download**.

- In the new window, select the format **FBX** for Unity (**.fbx**), leave all the other options as default, and then click on the button **Download**.

Figure 2-3: Setting the download options

- The browser will ask you where you would like to download this file.

- You may notice the name of the file: **dreyar_m_aure@Idle.fbx**.

- Please save the file to a location of your choice.

- Navigate to where you downloaded this asset and drag and drop it to the **Project** folder in Unity.

Note that you could, if you wished, create a new folder in Unity's Project window, to store all the animations that you have created.

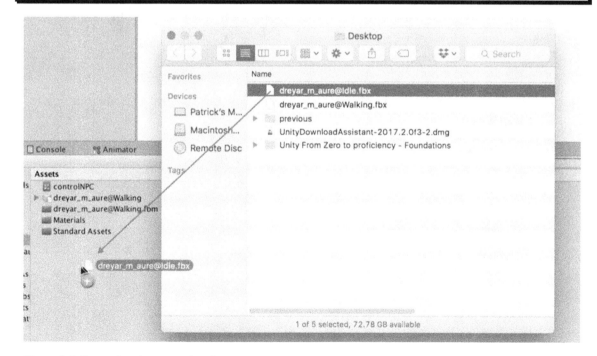

Figure 2-4: Importing the new animation

- This should create a new asset called **dreyar_m_aure@Idle** in the **Project** window.

- Please click on this asset in the **Project** window.

- In the **Inspector** window, click on the tab called **Model**, and change the attribute called **Scale Factor** to **0.1**; this will help to ensure that the animation is proportionate to the initial character imported earlier in Unity.

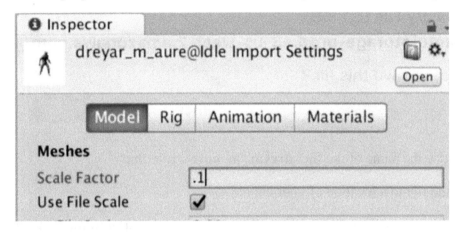

Figure 2-5: Modifying the scaling factor

- Click on the button labelled **Apply** to apply this change.

We will now, as we have done for the previous animation, ensure that the animation is looping:

- Please click on the tab called **Animation**.

- Scroll down in the **Inspector** window, and tick the box for the attribute called **Loop Time**.

- Press the button labeled **Apply**.

Once this is done, we can go back to the **Animator** window to create an additional state.

- Please open the **Animator** window (**Window | Animator**).

- You will see that, by default, the character should "go" straight to the state called walking by default, as per the next figure.

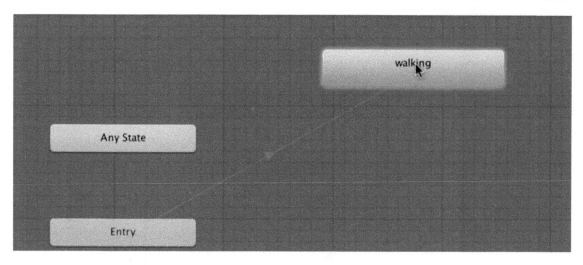

Figure 2-6: Modifying the animator controller

However, we would like the character to be initially idle, and then for this character to start walking based on a specific condition. For this purpose, we will rename the state called **walking** and also create a new state as follows:

- Please select the state called **walking**.

- Using the **Inspector** window, rename this state **idle**.

- Change the **Motion** attribute (or the animation) for this state to **Idle**: click on the cowheel to the left of the label **Motion**, and search and select the animation called **Idle** in the search window.

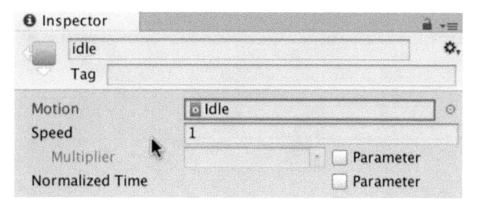

Figure 2-7: Adding an idle state

- Once this is done, you can test the scene and ensure that the character is in the **idle** state and that the animation is played indefinitely (i.e., looping).

Figure 2-8: Checking the state idle

Once that you have checked that the correct animation is applied, we will now create a new state and specify transitions between these states and conditions for these transitions to occur.

CREATING STATES AND TRANSITIONS

In this section we will look at parameters, transitions and conditions for the transition to complete.

As you open the **Inspector** window, you will see that we have a state called **idle**; so, in the next paragraphs, we will create another state called **walking**, along with transitions between these two states.

- Please create a new state: right-click on the canvas and then select: **Create State | Empty** for the contextual menu.

- Select this state (i.e., click on it), and, using the **Inspector**, change its name to **walking**.

- Using the **Motion** field for this state, set the associated animation for this state to **Walking**, as we have done previously.

At present, we would like to create a transition from the state **idle** to the state **walking**, so that our character can switch between these two states. So let's create this transition:

- Please right-click on the state called **idle**.

- From the contextual menu, choose the option **Make Transition**, as described in the next figure.

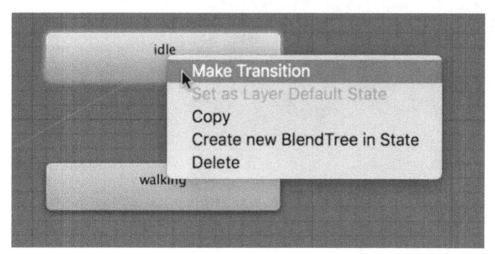

Figure 2-9: Creating a transition between states

You can then move the mouse and then click on the state called **walking**: this will create an arrow between the states that symbolizes a transition from the state **idle** to the state **walking**.

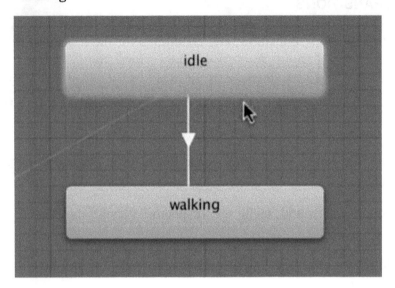

Figure 2-10: Completing the transition between two states

This transition means that whenever the idle animation has completed once, the game will automatically transition to the state called **walking**. If you play the scene, you should see that the **idle** mode will be active for a few seconds, and that the game will then transition to the state **idle** automatically.

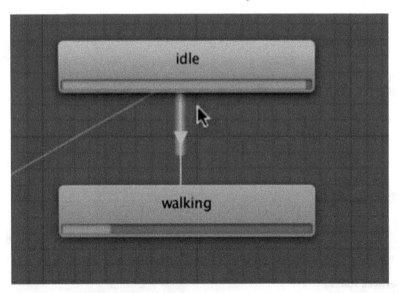

Figure 2-11: The game transitioning to the second state

So we have created transition without a condition, which means that this transition will be completed all the time. However, in our case, we would like this transition to occur only when a specific condition is fulfilled, for example, when the player presses the arrow key on the keyboard. This condition can be based on what is called a **parameter**, which is comparable to a variable associated to the **Animator Controller**. We could then check whether the value of this parameter is true or false to be able to proceed with the transition. So let's modify this transition:

- Please left-click on the transition between the states **idle** and **walking**.

- In the **Inspector** window, you will see a section called **Conditions**, with an empty list, which means that no conditions have been set for this transition yet, and that this transition will happen all the time.

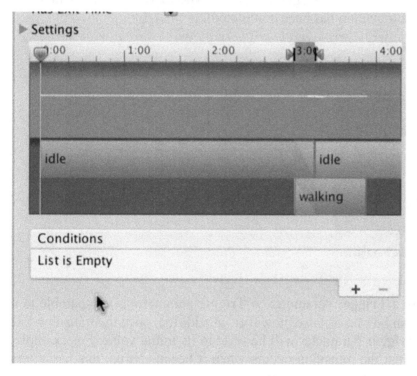

Figure 2-12: Checking the conditions for the transition

So, in our case, we will need to create a condition; for this purpose, we will first create a parameter, and then specify the value for this parameter that should trigger the transition.

- In the **Animator** window, please click on the tab called **Parameters**.

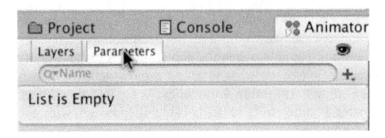

Figure 2-13: Accessing the parameters

- Click on the + button, to the right of the empty search field, this should display a list of possible types for the new parameter to be created: **Float** (float value), **Int** (Integer), **Bool** (Boolean) and **Trigger** (a special type of Boolean for which the value is reset after a transition has been completed).

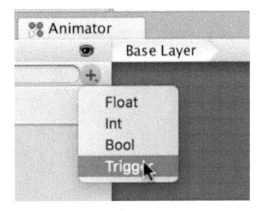

Figure 2-14: Selecting a type for the parameter

For our game, we will use a **Trigger** parameter. A Trigger parameter is comparable to a Boolean in that its value can be true or false; however, in addition, once the transition has occurred, the value of a **Trigger** parameter will be reset to its initial value. For example, if it is initially false, and that the transition occurs when it becomes true, this parameter will be reset to false after the transition, and vice-versa.

- Please select the option **Trigger**, this will create a new parameter.

- Rename this parameter **startWalking**, by double clicking on its name. By default, this parameter will be set to **false**.

- In the **Animator** window, click on the transition between the states **idle** and **walking**.

- Click on the + button to the right of the label "**List is Empty**".

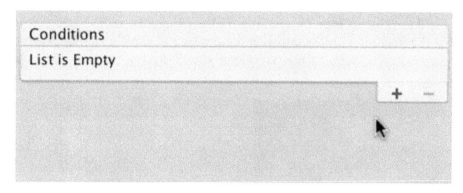

Figure 2-15: Adding a new transition (part 1)

- By default, it will add the parameter **isWalking** as the condition for the transition. This means that the transition will occur if this parameter is **true**. This parameter was chosen automatically because this is the only parameter available in the **Animator Controller** for now.

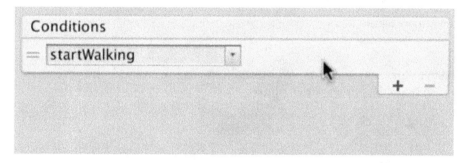

Figure 2-16: Adding a new transition (part 2)

- If you play the scene again, you will see that the character is in the **idle** state. Based on our previous change, the transition will not occur unless the parameter **isWalking** is set to true.

- Using the **Animator** window, you can check that the value of the parameter **isWalking** is false, as the radio button associated to it is not active.

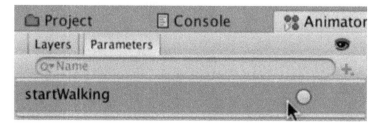

Figure 2-17: Checking the value of the parameter during the game

- Now, if you set this value to **true** by clicking on the associated radio button, you should see that the transition will occur; this is because, we have specified, early-on, that the transition will occur if the parameter **startWalking** is **true**, which is the case now.

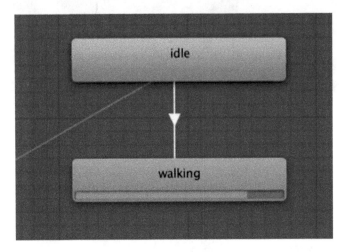

Figure 2-18: The states after the transition

You may also observe that as soon as the transition has occurred the parameter **isWalking** is now set to **false**, as per the next figure.

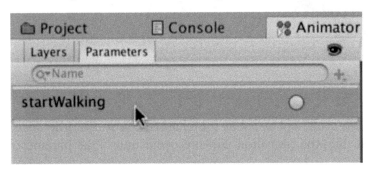

Figure 2-19: The Trigger parameter after the transition

Following what we have done previously, we will now create a transition from the state **walking** to the state **idle**, so that the character goes back to the idle mode when a parameter **stopWalking**, that we yet have to create, is false.

- Please create a new transition, this time, from the state **walking** to the state **idle**.

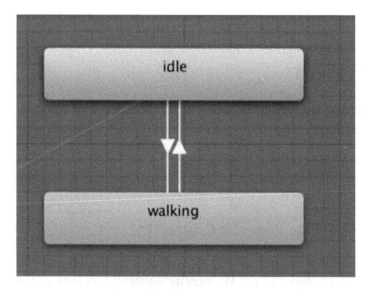

Figure 2-20: Creating a transition between walking and idle

- Create a new **Trigger** parameter called **stopWalking**.

- Select the transition that you have just created (from walking to **idle**), and use the parameter **stopWalking** as a condition for this condition to occur.

To test this new parameter, please play the scene, and successively click on the parameter **startWalking** and **stopWalking** in the **Animator** window, you should see that the character goes from the state idle to **walking**, and then back to the state **idle**.

Now, if we had used a Boolean value for the parameter **startWalking** and **stopWalking**, the transitions between these states would occur indefinitely, and you may try it yourself; this is the reason why, we have used Trigger variables in this case, so that after the transition, these parameters be reset to their original value.

Once we have these transitions working, the next step would be to modify the parameters, but this time from a script, so that we can associate these triggers to keys on the keyboard for instance, for the player to start or stop walking, and this will be done in the next section.

CONTROLLING STATES FROM A SCRIPT

In the last section, we managed to create transitions between different states, and what we will do for now is to control these from our script.

We will create a simple C# script to capture the keys pressed by the player and then connect these to the **Animator Controller** to be able to trigger transitions and ultimately control the 3D character.

- In Unity, please create a new C# script, and call it **ControlNPC**.

- Drag and drop this script on the **NPC** object that is available in the **Hierarchy** window. If you then click on this object in the **Hierarchy** window and look at the **Inspector**, you should now see that the Script **ControlNPC** has become a component of this object.

- Open this script by double-clicking on it. This should open your script in the default code editor (e.g., Visual Studio).

- Please type the following code in the script (new code in bold).

```
using System.Collections;

using System.Collections.Generic;

using UnityEngine;


public class ControlNPC : MonoBehaviour {

    Animator anim;

    AnimatorStateInfo info;

    // Use this for initialization

    void Start () {

        anim = GetComponent<Animator> ();

    }


    // Update is called once per frame

    void Update () {

        info = anim.GetCurrentAnimatorStateInfo(0);

        if (info.IsName ("idle"))

            print ("We are in the idle mode");

        if (info.IsName ("walking"))

            print ("We are in the walking mode");

    }

}
```

In the previous code:

- We declare two variables: the variable **anim** of type **Animator** that will point to the **Animator Controller** linked to the 3D character, and the variable called **info** that will be used to determine the current state.

- In the **Start** function we mention that the variable **anim** points to the **Animator** linked to this 3D character.

- In the **Update** method, we link the variable **info** to the first layer of the animator that we have defined previously, hence the number **0** at the end of the next code snippet (the first layer has the index **0**, the second layer has the index **1**, and so on...).

```
anim.GetCurrentAnimatorStateInfo(0);
```

- By default, and as illustrated in the next figure, the **Animator Controller** includes only one layer named **Base Layer**.

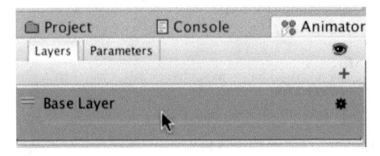

Figure 2-21: The default layer for the Animator Controller

- We then access this **Animator Controller** and check the name if its current state.

- If the current state is **idle** then we display the message **"we are in the idle state"**; otherwise, we display the message **"we are in the state walking"**.

Once this is done, we can start to use this script to control the NPC from the **Animator** window.

- Please save your script.

- Switch to Unity, and play the scene.

- Open the console window and click on the tab called **collapse**, so that it is easier to see the messages printed in this window.

Figure 2-22: Collapsing the messages

- As the scene is playing, you should see that the message **"we are in the idle mode"** is displayed.

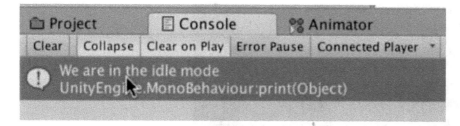

Figure 2-23: Displaying messages in the idle mode

You may also notice a number displayed to the right of the window, to specify how many times this message has been displayed, as illustrated in the next figure. This is because this message is displayed from the **Update** method and that it would usually be printed indefinitely in this state, if we had not selected the option called **Collapse**.

Figure 2-24: Collapsed messages

- You can now click on the **Animation** tab.

- Then click on the tab called **Parameters**.

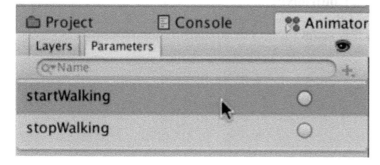

Figure 2-25: Opening the Animator window

- Click on the radio button for the parameter **startWalking**.

- You should see that the **Animator Controller** is now in the walking state, as illustrated in the next figure.

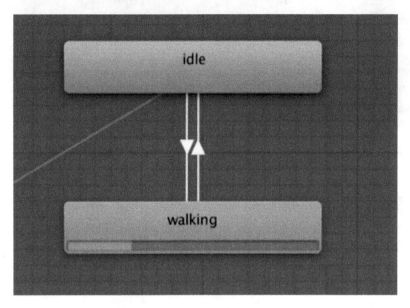

Figure 2-26: Switching to the walking state

- If you switch to the **Console** window, you should now see a message saying "**we are in the walking state**".

Now what we could do, is to trigger a transition, but this time, from the code.

- Please open the script called **ControlNPC**.

- Add the following code to this script (new code in bold).

```
void Update () {

    info = anim.GetCurrentAnimatorStateInfo(0);

    if (info.IsName ("idle"))

        print ("We are in the idle mode");

    if (info.IsName ("walking"))

        print ("We are in the walking mode");

        if(Input.GetKey (KeyCode.P)) anim.SetTrigger
("startWalking");

        if (Input.GetKey (KeyCode.O)) anim.SetTrigger
("stopWalking");


}
```

In the previous code:

- We check which key was pressed by the user.

- If the **P** key is pressed, then we set the Trigger variable **startWalking**.

- If the O key is pressed, then we set the Trigger variable **stopWalking**.

You can now save your code and go back to Unity, play the scene, click in the **Game** window (so that keys can be detected), and do the following:

- Make sure that the **Animator** window is visible.

- Press the **P** key on your keyboard.

- You should notice that the parameter **startWalking** is briefly set to true and that the NPC is now in the state called **walking**. Remember, because this parameter is a **Trigger** variable, it will be reset to its default value (i.e., false) once the transition has occurred.

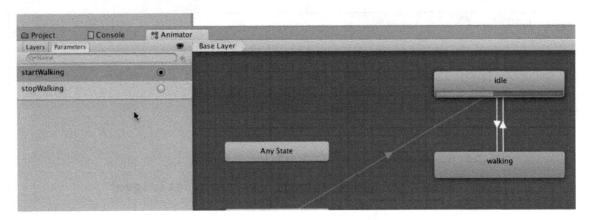

Figure 2-27: The startWalking parameter is set to true

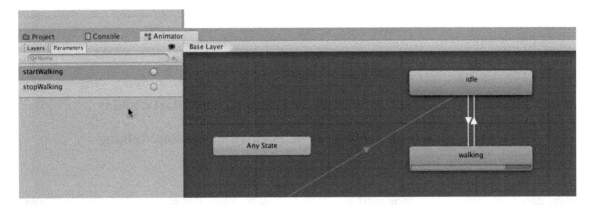

Figure 2-28: The transition to the state walking occurs and the parameter is set back to false.

You can then press the **O** key on your keyboard, and you should see, that as for the previous case, the parameter **stopWalking** will briefly be set to true, the transition to the state **idle** will occur, and the parameter **stopWalking** will be reset to false.

So, in this section, you have managed to control the NPC's states from the keyboard, using a script that accesses the **Animator Controller** and that sets the values of its parameter. In the next section we will get to move the character around using a similar principle.

LEVEL ROUNDUP

Well, this is it!

In this chapter, we have learned about Finite State Machines. We have created an Animator Controller, along with states and parameters. We have also linked these states to the 3D character and to the animations that we have created earlier. Along the way, we have learned how to create transition between these states, and how to control them using the Animator window, or through a C# script that checks for the keys pressed by the player. So, we have, again, covered some significant ground compared to the last chapter. Well done!

Checklist

You can consider moving to the next chapter if you can do the following:

- Create an Animator Controller.

- Create States and parameters.

- Create transitions between states, and control them through a script

Quiz

Now, let's check your knowledge! Please answer the following questions or specify if these statements are either correct or incorrect (the solutions are on the next page).

1. A **Trigger** parameter will be reset to its default value after a transition.

2. A **Boolean** parameter will be reset to its default value after a transition.

3. By default, an **Animator Controller** has two layers.

4. It is possible to access the **Animator** component linked to an object from C#.

5. It is possible to know the current state for a specific **Animator Controller** through C#.

6. It is possible to set the value of a **Trigger** parameter from C# using the method **SetTriggerParameter**.

7. The method **GetCurrentAnimatorStateInfo** can be used to determine the current state for an **Animator Controller**.

8. By default, an **Animator** component includes an **Animator Controller**.

9. An Animator component is necessary to be able to animate a 3D character.

10. For a given state, the attribute called **Motion** can be used to specify the animation that should be played in this state.

Quiz Solutions

Now, let's check if you have answered the questions correctly.

1. True.

2. False.

3. False (only one).

4. True.

5. True.

6. False (it is the method **SetTrigger**).

7. True.

8. False.

9. True.

10. True.

Challenge 1

Now that you have managed to complete this chapter please try the following:

- Create your own **Animator Controller**.

- Create three states: **state1**, **state2**, and **state3**.

- Create two **Trigger** parameters **param1** and **param2**.

- Create transitions from **state1** to **state2** and then from **state2** to **state3,** and associate each of these transitions with the parameters **param1** and **param2,** respectively.

- Add the **Animator Controller** to an empty object, and test the transition by changing the parameters in the **Animator** window.

3

USING 1-DIMENSIONAL BLEND TREES

In the previous section, we added and controlled a character using the keys O and P. We controlled the transitions between states using the parameters **startWalking** and **stopWalking**.

In this section we will be using a combination of the arrow keys and what is called a **Character Controller** that will help us to move our character around our scene. We will also use blend trees so that we can smoothly transition from the states **idle**, to the state **walking** and then to the state **running**.

So, in this section, we will start to look at the following:

- Blend Trees.

- Character Controllers.

- Modifying the speed of an animation.

After completing this chapter, you will be able to:

- Create and apply a **1D blend** tree to your character.

- Apply smooth transitions between the animations **idle**, **walk** and **run** based on the speed of the character.

- Reverse the speed of an animation so that the character walks backwards.

The code solutions for this chapter are included in the **resource pack** that you can download by following the instructions included in the section entitled "Support and Resources for this Book".

ADDING NEW ANIMATIONS

In the next sections, we will create a smooth transition between the animations **idle**, **walk**, and **run**.

If you would prefer not to use Mixamo to create your animations, theses animations are available in your resource pack that you can download by following the instructions included in the section entitled "**Support and Resources for this Book**".

First, we will need to create a new animation for when the character is running as follows.

- Please open the Mixamo page: **http://www.mixamo.com**.

- Once you are logged-in, click on the tab called **Animations**.

- Using the search field, search for animations that include the word **running**.

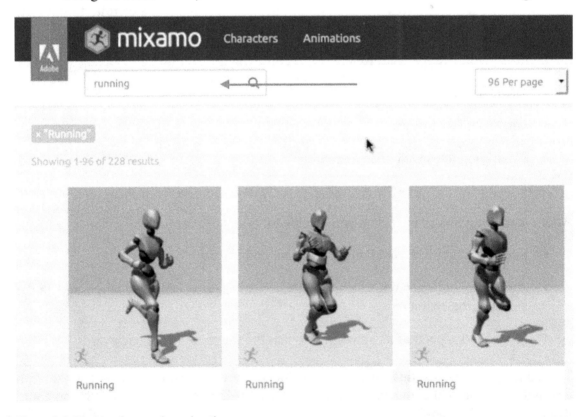

Figure 3-1: Looking for running animations

- You can select any animation of your choice by clicking on it; for this example, I have chosen the first one (i.e., top-left animation).

- Once the animation is applied, your character on the right hand of the screen should appear with a running animation, as per the next figure.

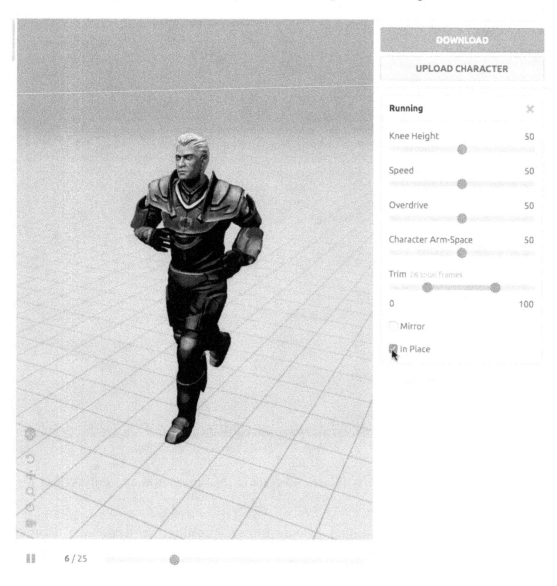

Figure 3-2: Applying a running animation

- Once this is done, you can download your animated character, as you have done with the previous animations, by clicking on the button called "**Download**" after selecting the format "**FBX for Unity**".

CREATING A BLEND TREE

Once your animation has been created and saved to your hard drive, you can import it to Unity by dragging and dropping this file from your system to Unity.

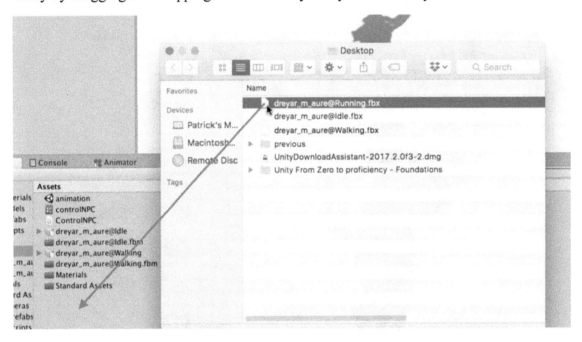

Figure 3-3: Importing the new animation

Once this is done, a new asset called **dreyar_aure@Running.fbx** should be created in your **Project** window.

As for the other animations, we will need to rescale this animation and ensure that it is looping.

- Please select the asset called **dreyar_aure@Running.fbx** from your **Project** window.

- Using the **Inspector**, click on the tab called **Model**.

- Modify the attribute **Scale Factor** to **0.1**.

- Click on the button labeled **Apply** to apply your changes.

- Click on the tab called **Animations**.

- Select the option **Loop Time** and press the button labelled **Apply**.

Once this is done, our animation is ready to be used.

It is now time to create our blend tree.

- Please select the object called **NPC** in the **Hierarchy** window.

- Open the **Animator** window.

- Remove the transitions between the state **idle** and the state **walking**: click on each of the transitions and then press the **DELETE** key on your keyboard.

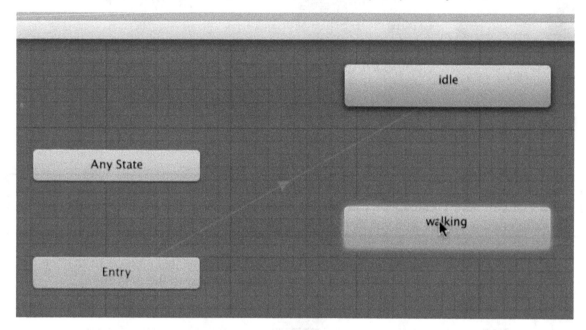

Figure 3-4: Deleting transitions

- Right-click on the canvas, and select: **Create State | From New Blend Tree**, as per the next figure.

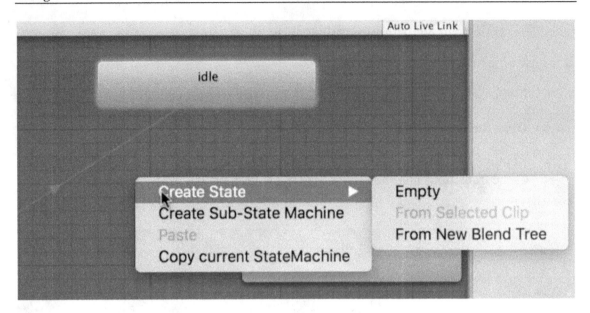

Figure 3-5: Adding a blend tree

Note that because the Animator window will rapidly become cluttered with the different states that you have created, you can pan the view by pressing the **ALT** key and dragging and dropping the mouse, you can also zoom in and out using the mouse wheel.

- Please double click on the new blend tree that you have just created so that we can edit its content; this should open a new window similar to the next figure.

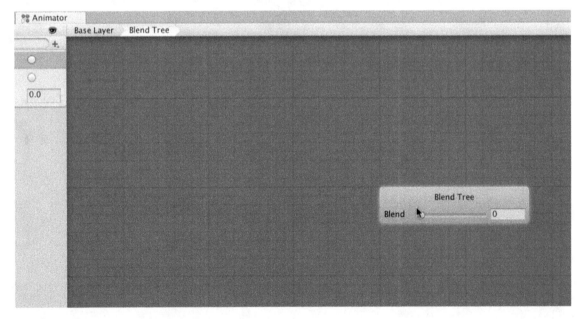

Figure 3-6: Configuring the blend tree

This blend tree will be used to blend between animations based on the value of a given parameter. In our case, we will blend the animation **idle**, **walking** and **running** based on the speed of the character; so we will create parameter called **speed** accordingly.

- In the **Animator** window, click on the tab called **Parameters** and then on the + sign to the right of the search field to create a **Float** parameter, as per the next figure.

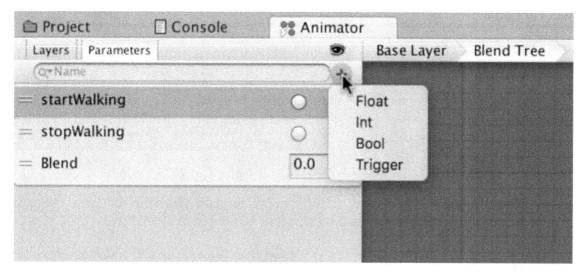

Figure 3-7: Creating a new parameter

- Select the blend tree in the canvas.

- Using the **Inspector** window, select the parameter called **speed** for the attribute called **Parameter**; this means that the blend tree will branch to a specific animation based on the value of the parameter called **speed**.

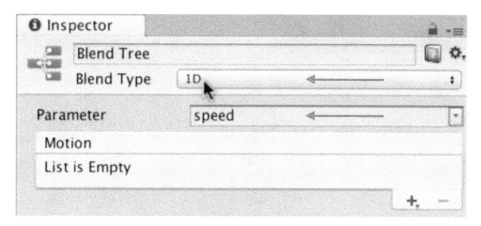

Figure 3-8: Selecting a 1-Dimensional blend tree

You may notice that the **Blend Type**, in the **Inspector** window, is **1D**, meaning that the branching or transition will occur only based on one parameter; as we will see later, it is also possible to create **2-Dimensional** blend trees, where the branching or transitions are based on two parameters (hence the name 2-Dimensional).

You may also notice that the blend tree now includes a slider with the label **speed**; and if you move this slider from left to right, you will see that the value of the parameter **speed** will vary from 0 to 1.

So at this stage, we have managed to create a blend tree, and to specify that its transitions will be based on the parameter **speed**.

The next step will be to specify the animations or branches to be included in the blend tree; in other words, we will specify what animations should be played based on the value of the parameter called **speed**.

- Please right-click on the blend tree.

- From the contextual menu select the option **Add Motion**; this will make it possible to include the animations that will be used in our blend tree.

- Please repeat the previous step twice, so that you effectively add three possible **Motions**.

- As you do so, you should notice three dots aligned vertically, to the right of the blend tree, as illustrated in the next figure.

Figure 3-9: Adding Motions

- Each of these dots corresponds to a potential animation for our blend tree.

- If you look at the **Inspector** window, you should also see that three corresponding fields have been created accordingly.

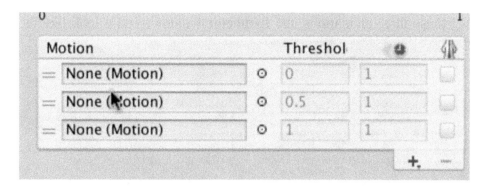

Figure 3-10: Adding new Motions for the blend tree

So each of the dots that you use on the blend tree correspond to one of the three potential **Motions** for the blend tree.

The idea of this blend tree is that we will specify three animations and thresholds that will indicate when to transition from (or blend between) one animation and the next. This threshold is related to the value of the parameter called **speed**.

As you can see, each of the **Motion** fields in the **Inspector** window is empty, and we will need to specify corresponding animations.

- Please click on the cogwheel located to the right of the first empty field; this should open a new window labeled **Select Motion** from where you can select an animation.

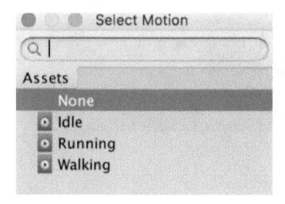

Figure 3-11: Selecting an animation

- Please select the animation called **Idle**.

- You can now repeat the previous step so that the second **Motion** filed uses the animation called **Walking**, and so that the third **Motion** field uses the animation called **Running**.

- After adding these three animations, the **Inspector** window should look like the next figure.

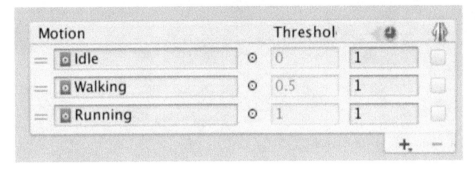

Figure 3-12: Adding three animations

- The blend tree in the canvas should look like the following figure.

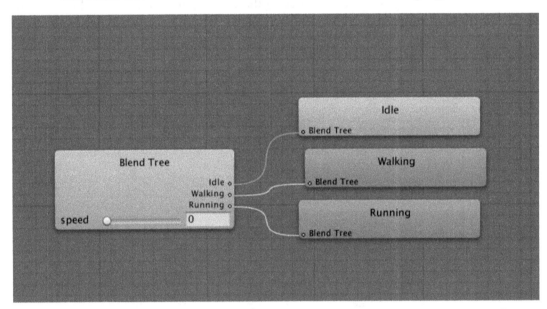

Figure 3-13: The blend tree with three animations

The idea of the blend tree is that, depending on the value of the parameter **speed**, and on the threshold (that we yet need to set-up), the blend tree will branch out to the **Idle**, **Walking** or **Running** animation.

So, at this stage, we just need to specify the different thresholds for the **speed** parameter.

- Using the **Inspector** window, please untick the box called **Automate Thresolds**; this will make it possible for us to set each threshold manually.

- Set a Threshold of **0.4** for the animation **Idle**, **0.7** for the animation **Walking**, and **0.9** for the animation **Running**, as per the next figure.

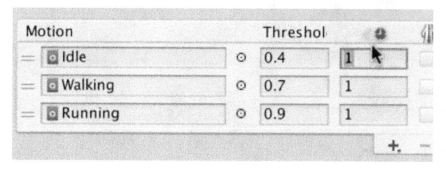

Figure 3-14: Setting the thresholds for the animations

The second column labeled **Thresold** will set the threshold for each animation. So based on these values, Unity will use 100% of the animation **Idle** when the speed is **0.4**, 100% of the animation **Walking** wen the speed is **0.7** and 100% of the animation **Running** wen the speed is **.9**. When the speed falls between these values, Unity will perform blending between the corresponding animation; for example, if the speed is **.55** (i.e., half way between **.4** and **.7**), 50% of each of the animation **Idle** and **Walking** will be used.

The third column is dedicated to the speed of the animation; **1** meaning that the animation is played normally, and **-1** that the animation is played at normal speed but in reverse. For example, using the **Walking** animation with a parameter **-1** in the second column, would cause the animation to be played in reverse, meaning that the character would look like it is walking backwards.

You can test your blend tree by just moving the slider on the blend tree that corresponds to the parameter **speed**. As you increase the speed, you should see that different animations are highlighted in the **Blend Tree**, as per the next figure.

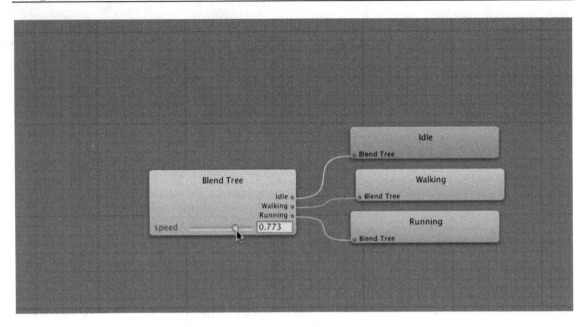

Figure 3-15: Blending between animations

For example, in the previous figure, both **Walking** and **Running** are highlighted, and the connection to the animation **Walking** is blue; this means that because the speed is **0.773**, that the current animation is **Walking**, and Unity is blending between this animation and then next one (i.e., **Running**).

You can also check the preview of the animation at the bottom of the **Inspector** window, as per the next figure.

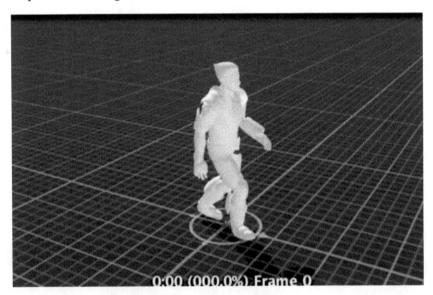

Figure 3-16: Checking the blending between animations

- You can now exit the blend tree by clicking on the tab **Base Layer**.

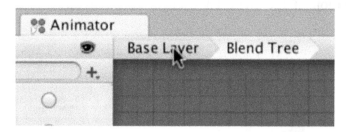

Figure 3-17: Switching between the base Layer and the Blend Tree

You can now create a transition between the state **idle** and the blend tree (right-click on the state **idle**, and select **Make Transition**). This means that we will go straight from the **idle** state to the blend tree. Once in the blend tree, Unity will decide as to which animation should be played depending on the parameter called **speed**.

We can now test our settings.

- Please play the scene.

- Looking at the **Animator** window, you should see that it transitions to the blend tree immediately, as per the next figure.

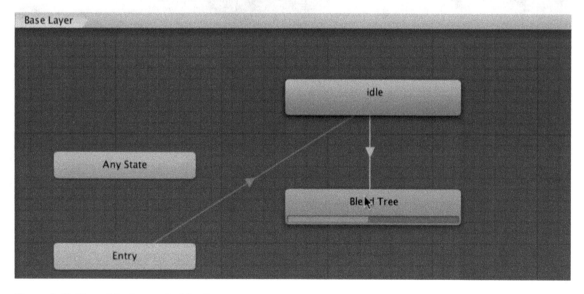

Figure 3-18: Transitioning to the blend tree

- Double click on the blend tree.

- You can then increase the value of the parameter speed manually by moving the slider and see how the animation of the character changes in the **Scene** or the **Game** view.

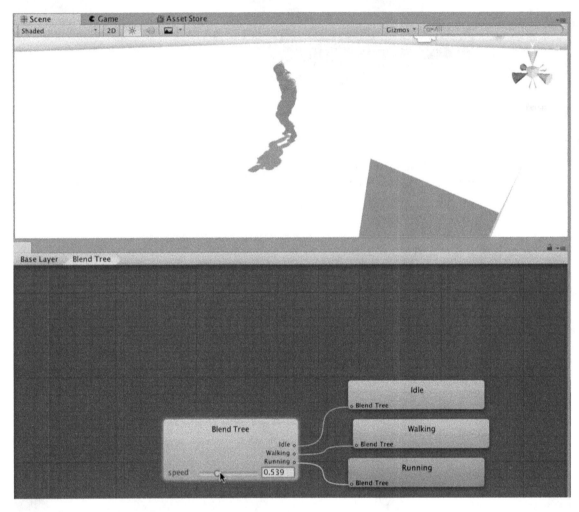

Figure 3-19: Controlling the tree while the game is played

CONTROLLING A BLEND TREE FROM A SCRIPT

In the previous section we created a blend tree and a parameter called **speed** that could be increased to progressively blend between the animations. At this stage, we will create some code that will ensure that the speed can be controlled by pressing a key on the keyboard.

If you remember well, we managed to create a script in the previous section that detected the keys **P** and **O** to be able to trigger the parameter **startWalking** and **stopWalking,** and we will proceed similarly for our blend tree.

- Please open the script **ControlNPC**.

- Comment the following lines:

```
/*if(Input.GetKey (KeyCode.P)) anim.SetTrigger ("startWalking");
if (Input.GetKey (KeyCode.O)) anim.SetTrigger ("stopWalking");*/
```

- Please add this code at the start of the class.

```
float speed;
```

We will try to detect the arrows pressed on the keyboard and then map these to the variable called speed.

- Please add this code to the **Update** method.

```
speed = Input.GetAxis ("Vertical");
anim.SetFloat ("speed", speed);
```

In the previous code:

- The vertical axis ranges from -1 to 1 (i.e., left key or right key).

- So in this case we detect whether the up or down keys are pressed.

- We then set the parameter **speed** in the **Animator Controller** with this value.

Please save the script; you can now play the scene, click in the **Game** view and press the up arrow, you should see that the parameter called **speed** increases to 1.

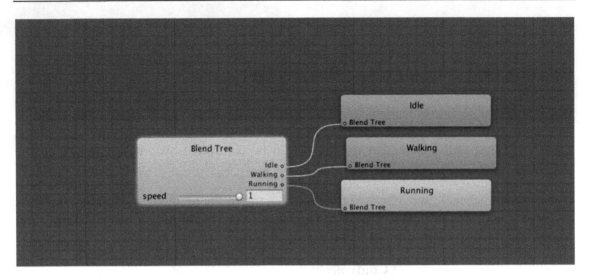

Figure 3-20: Increasing the speed using the keyboard

As you release the up arrow key, the speed will decrease to 0; and again if you press the down arrow, the speed will decrease to **-1** and then back to **0** as you release this key.

So at this stage, it works in the sense that we have managed to control the animation from the arrow keys. However, the character is not moving forward, so we will need to modify the script and to also add what is called a **Character Controller** to the 3D Character.

COMBINING A CHARACTER CONTROLLER AND A BLEND TREE

In this section, we will make sure that our character is moving forward as the blending occurs between the different animations. So far we have seen that the speed can be controlled using the up and down arrow keys; however, now, we would like to move the character forward. So we will add a character controller, a component that is often useful to move a character in a 3D environment from a script.

- Please select the object called **NPC** in the **Hierarchy**.

- In the **Inspector** window, click on the button called **Add Component**.

- Type the text **control** in the search field; this will show you the available components for which the name includes the word **control**.

- Select **Character Controller** from the list of options, as per the next figure.

Figure 3-21: Adding a Character Controller component

- Once the **Character Controller** has been added, you can leave all its parameters as they are, except from the center of the character controller.

- If you look at the **Scene View**, you should see a green capsule that corresponds to the **Character Controller**; this capsule should encapsulate the full character, however, at the moment, its position is too low, so its y-coordinate needs to be changed.

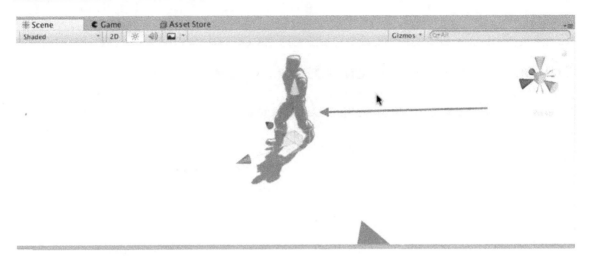

Figure 3-22: The Character Controller with the default options

- In the **Inspector** window, change the y-coordinate of the center of the Character Controller to **1**. You should then see that now the capsule covers the full character, as per the next figure.

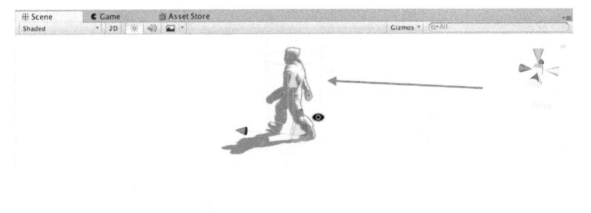

Figure 3-23: The Character Controller after the changes

The next things we need to do is to declare and use the **Character Controller** in our script, so that the NPC can be move forward.

- Please open the script called **ControlNPC**.

- Add the following code at the beginning of the class.

```
CharacterController control;
```

- Add the following code in the **Start** function (new code in bold).

```
void Start ()
{

    anim = GetComponent<Animator> ();

    control = GetComponent<CharacterController> ();

}
```

In the previous code, we link our variable called **control** to the **Character Controller** component that has previously been added to the NPC.

The idea behind the character controller is that you can move it or rotate it from a script as we will see in the next section.

- Please add the following code to the **Update** function:

```
control.SimpleMove (transform.forward * speed);
```

In the previous code: we use the built-in method **SimpleMove** to move the character forward using the speed that is controlled by the up and arrow keys. Note that the method needs a **Vector3** variable to know in which direction the NPC should be moved; this direction, in the previous code, is provided by the **forward** vector from the current object (i.e., the NPC); this vector is multiplied by the speed, so that the higher the speed and the faster the character will move forward.

You can now save your code and play the scene. As you click in the **Game** view and press the **up arrow key**, you should see that the character is actually moving forward (i.e., running), as per the next figure.

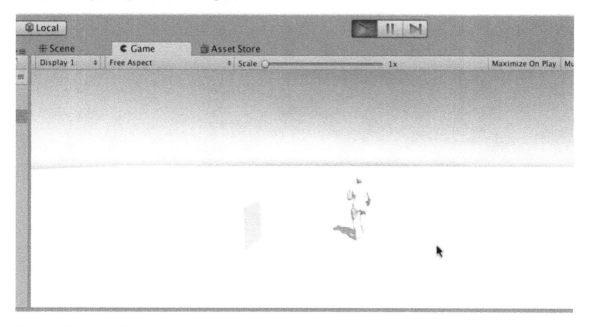

Figure 3-24: Controlling the character through a script

As you are playing the scene, you may see that if you press the **down arrow**, the character is translating backwards, but with no associated animations, and that is perfectly normal for now, as we have not defined any animation for when the variable speed is negative, and we will do that in the next sections.

ROTATING THE CHARACTER

While in the previous section we moved the character forward by increasing the value of parameter **speed**, in this section we will be using a similar concept to be able to rotate the character by pressing the left and right arrows on the keyboard.

- Please open the script called **ControlNPC**.

- Add the following statement at the beginning of the class.

```
float rotationAngle;
```

The variable **rotationAngle** will be used to determine the rotation angle for the character.

- Please add the following code to the **Update** function.

```
rotationAngle - Input.GetAxis("Horizontal");
transform.Rotate(0, rotationAngle, 0);
```

In the previous code:

- We detect whether the left or right arrows on the keyboard were pressed, and save the corresponding values (i.e., **-1** for left, **1** for right, or **0** when both keys are released).

- Note that we use the **Horizontal** axis this time as we are interested in the left and right arrow keys.

- We then rotate the object around the y axis using an angle with the value of the variable **rotationAngle**.

You can now save your code and play the scene. After clicking once on the **Game** view, and pressing the up and right arrows, you will see that the character will start walking forward, and that it will also turn to the right.

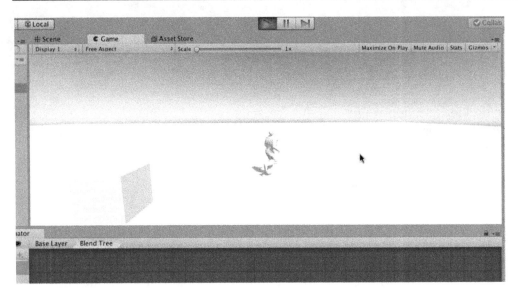

Figure 3-25: Moving forward and turning to the right

REVERSING THE SPEED OF ANIMATIONS

In the previous, section we managed to move and to rotate the character through the keyboard and to also employ a blend tree to blend between animations; however, if you try to move the character back using the down arrow key, you will see that the character is going backward, but with no corresponding animation. So it would be better for the character to walk in reverse as the value of the parameter called **speed** is negative.

The idea to solve this issue, is to create a new state for the **Animator Controller**, and to play the **walking** animation backward for this specific state. So let's proceed:

- Please select the **NPC** object.

- Open the **Animator** window.

- Open the blend tree (i.e., double-click on the blend tree).

- Right-click on the blend tree and select the option **Add Motion** as per the next figure.

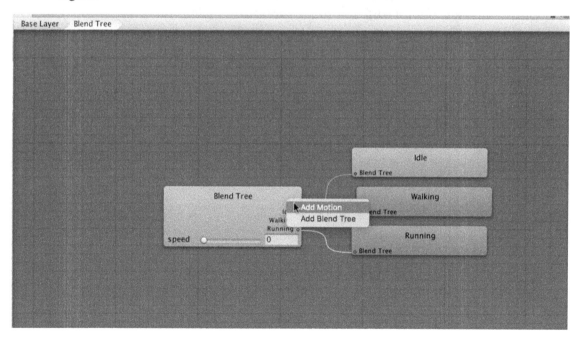

Figure 3-26: Adding a new Motion

- This should create a new empty **Motion** in the **Inspector** window as well as a corresponding state in the canvas.

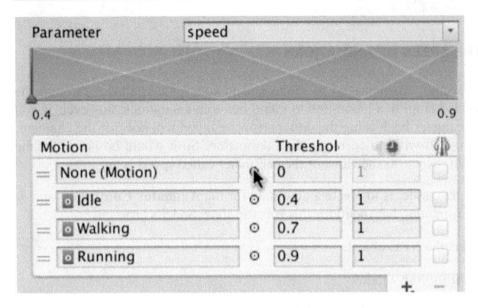

Figure 3-27: New empty Motion

- Click on the cogwheel to the right of the field with the text **None (Motion)** (as per the previous figure) and select the animation called **Walking** as per the next figure.

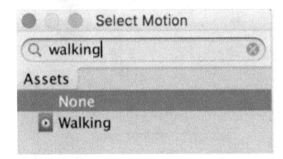

Figure 3-28: electing a new animation

- Set the animation speed to **-1** for this **Motion**, and a **Threshold** of **-.02**; this means that the animation called **Walking** will be played in reverse.

- Set the **Threshold** to **0** for the **Idle** Motion.

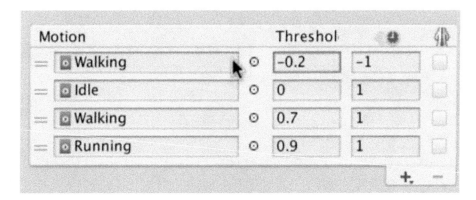

Figure 3-29: Setting the Threshold and speed for an animation

The **Animator Controller** should now look like the next figure:

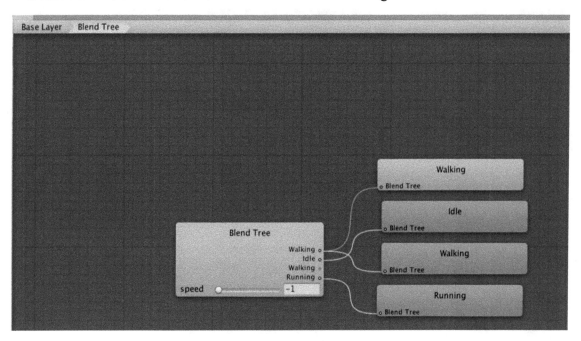

Figure 3-30: A new state has been created

- You can now play your scene and try to make the NPC walk backward and you should see that the **Walking** animation is played in reverse.

Figure 3-31: The NPC walking in reverse

LEVEL ROUNDUP

Well, this is it!

In this chapter, we have learned how to create 1D Blend trees to blend between animations. We also looked into modifying the speed of an animation so that it can be played in reverse. So, we have, again, covered some significant ground compared to the last chapter, and you should, by now, feel more comfortable with animations and blend trees.

Checklist

You can consider moving to the next chapter if you can do the following:

- Create a blend tree.

- Add Motions to a blend tree.

- Include thresholds for a specific blend tree.

- Reverse the speed of an animation.

Quiz

Now, let's check your knowledge! Please answer the following questions or specify if these statements are either correct or incorrect (the solutions are on the next page).

1. A blend tree blends between animations.

2. A 1D blend tree only needs one parameter to decide when the blending should occur.

3. A 1D blend tree only needs two parameters to decide when the blending should occur.

4. Only three Motions can be added to a blend tree.

5. A Threshold in a blend tree is used to specify when a speed too high for an animation.

6. A Threshold in a blend tree is used to decide when a transition (and the corresponding blending) should occur.

7. It is possible to control the blending parameter (for a blend tree) from a script.

8. The method **Input.GetAxis** returns a value between -1 and 1.

9. The method **Input.GetAxis** can be used to detect which arrow keys id pressed on the keyboard.

10. A character controller can be used to move a 3D character.

Quiz Solutions

Now, let's check if you have answered the questions correctly.

1. True.

2. True.

3. False.

4. False.

5. False.

6. True.

7. True.

8. True.

9. True.

10. True.

4
USING 2D BLEND TREES

In this section we will start to look at 2D blend trees and after completing this chapter, you will be able to:

- Create a 2D blend tree.

- Control a 2D blend tree from a script.

- Map the movement of your character to the arrow keys.

CREATING STRAFING ANIMATIONS

If you remember well, in the last section we used a blend tree to combine the animations **Walking**, **Idle**, and **Running**. This was a 1D blend tree based on the parameter called **speed**.

In this section, we will employ a blend tree that uses two parameters so that we can not only use the **Idle**, **Walking** and **Running** animations, but also to make it possible for the NPC to strafe to the left and to the right.

If you would prefer not to use Mixamo to create the new animations to be used in this section, these animations are available in the resource pack that you can download by following the instructions included in the section entitled "**Support and Resources for this Book**".

Before we start, we will create and download a strafing animation for our character:

- Using Mixamo, please open the **Animation** tab and search for animations for which the name includes the word **strafe**.

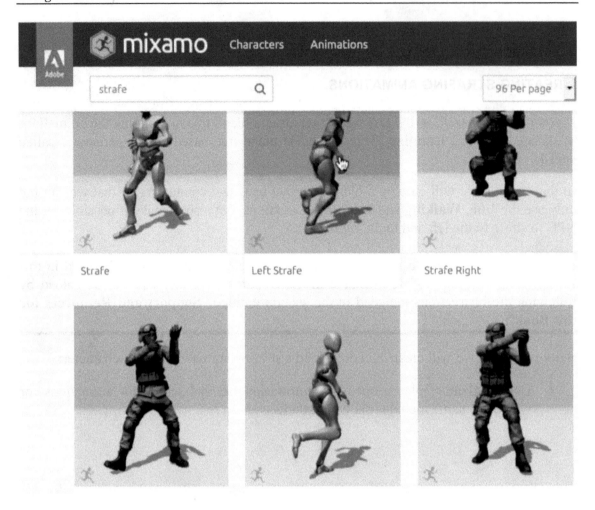

Figure 4-1: Looking for strafing animations

- Once Mixamo returns a list of the strafing animations, you can select the animation called **Walking Strafe Right** so that it is applied to your character.

Figure 4-2: Applying the strafing animation

- Once this is done, you can tick the box labelled **"In Place"** to the right of the Mixamo window. This is because we will move the character ourselves in Unity, so for now we only need the strafing animation to be "in place".

- You can then download the corresponding animation by clicking on the **"Download"** button, before saving it to your hard drive.

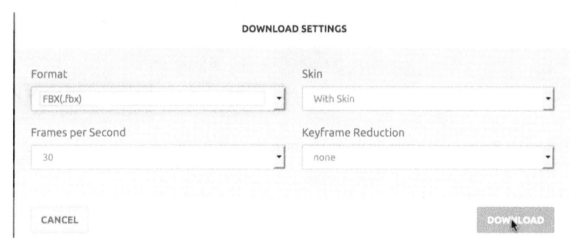

Figure 4-3: Downloading the animation

- You can then repeat the last two steps to create and save the animation called **Walk Strafe Left**.

CREATING A 2D BLEND TREE

At this stage, you probably have downloaded your two strafing animations **dreyar_m_aure@Walk Strafe Left** and **dreyar_m_aure@Walk Strafe Right**.

- Please import these to Unity by **dragging** and **dropping** them from your file system to the **Project** folder in Unity.

- You will need, as for the other animations, to adjust their size by selecting each of these assets in the **Project** window, and then use the tab call **Model** in the **Inspector** window to set their **Scale Factor** attribute to **.01**, as per the next figures.

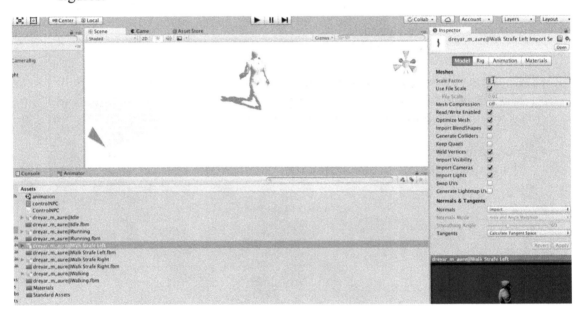

Figure 4-4: Adjusting the scale factor for the animated character

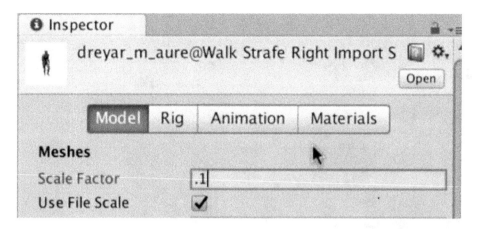

Figure 4-5: Setting the scale factor to 0.1

- You can also ensure that these are looping by selecting the tab called **Animation** in the **Inspector** before ticking the box labelled **Loop** time.

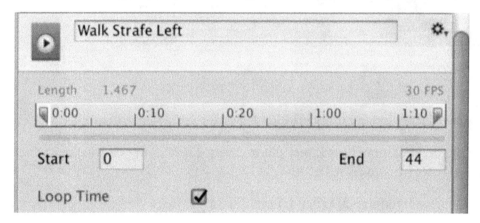

Figure 4-6: Setting the Loop Time option

- Please make sure that you modify both animations (i.e., **Walk Strafe Right** and **Walk Strafe Left**) so that their size and looping features are correct.

- You can now switch to the **Animator** window.

Because we will create another blend tree, you can, for the time being, remove the transition between the state **Idle** and the existing blend tree (i.e., click once on the transition and then press delete).

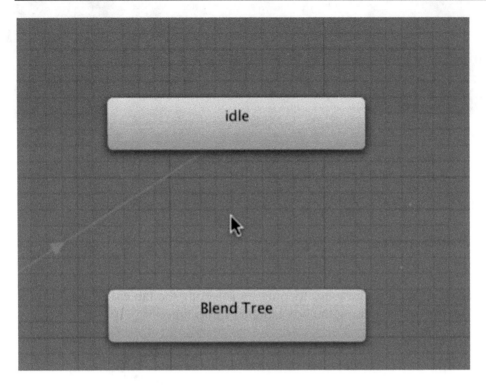

Figure 4-7: Deleting a transition

- You can also rename the previous **1D blend tree** for clarity.

- We can now create a new blend tree: please, right click in the canvas and select the option **Create | From New Blend Tree**.

- Rename this new blend tree **2D Blend Tree**.

- Open this blend tree by double clicking on it.

- In the **Inspector** window, select the option called **2D Simple Directional**, as per the next figure.

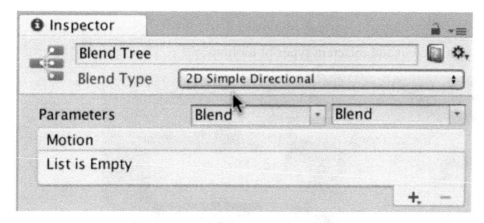

Figure 4-8: Selecting a 2D Simple Directional blend tree

As per the previous figure, there are two empty fields created for this blend tree that correspond to the parameters that can be used to blend animations in this tree.

So first, we will create these two parameters.

- In the **Animator** window, please click on the tab called **Parameters**.

- Create two **Float** parameters and rename them **xPos** and **yPos**.

- Once this is done, using the **Inspector** window, you can select these parameters for the blend tree to specify that the animation and the blending will be based on the parameters **xPos** and **yPos**.

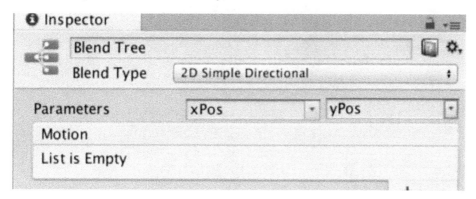

Figure 4-9: Specifying the parameters

At this stage, we just need to add different types of motions.

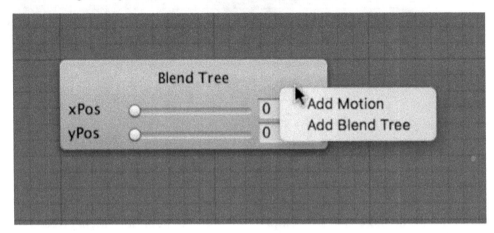

As we have done previously, right click on the blend tree (as per the previous figure), and select the option **Add Motion** several times to create the following:

- A motion with the animation **Walk Strafe Left**, with an **xPos** value of **-1** and a **yPos** value of **0**.

- A motion with the animation **Walk Strafe Right**, with an **xPos** value of **+1**.

As soon as you complete these two first motions, you should see a graphical representation of the parameters, using a plane, in the **Inspector** window as follows.

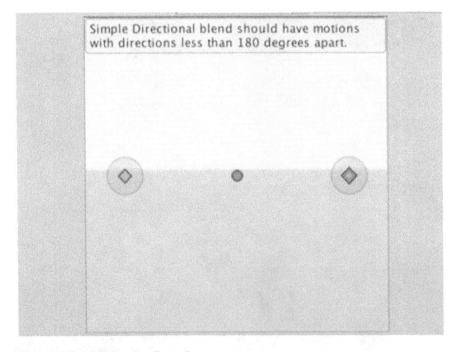

Figure 4-10: Mapping the xPos values.

Note that to add a **Motion** field, you can also click on the + button that is located in the bottom right corner of the **Inspector** window, as per the next figure.

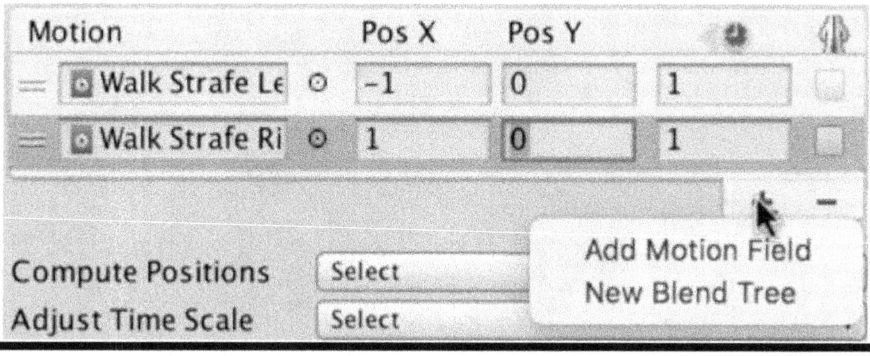

Figure 4-11: Adding a new motion field

You can now do the following:

- Please add a new **Motion** with the animation **Walking**, with an **yPos** value of **1** and a **xPos** value of **0**.

- Add a new **Motion** with the animation **Walking**, with an **yPos** value of **-1** and an animation speed of **-1** so that the **Walking** animation is played in reverse in this case.

- Finally, add a new **Motion** with the animation **Idle**, with an **yPos** value of **0** an **xPos** value of **0**, and an animation speed of **1**. This corresponds to the case where none of the arrow keys are pressed.

When you have finished adding the four animations, the **Inspector** window should look like the next figures.

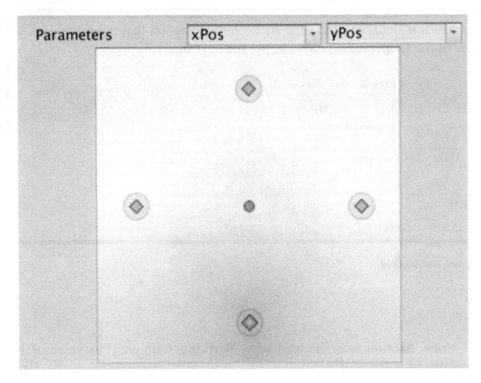

Figure 4-12: 2D mapping of the parameters

Motion	Pos X	Pos Y		
Walk Strafe L	-1	0	1	
Walk Strafe F	1	0	1	
Walking	0	1	1	
Walking	0	-1	-1	
Idle	0	0	1	

Figure 4-13: The new motions created

The arrow keys are mapped on a 2-Dimensional representation; so strafing to the left correspond to a position of **(-1,0)** on the 2D plane, strafing to the right correspond to a position of **(1,0)**, walking forward correspond to a position of **(0, 1)**, and walking back corresponds to a position of **(0, -1)** on this map.

Before we can test the scene, we just need to create a transition from the state **idle** to the state **2D Blend Tree**, so please create this transition with no specific condition.

Once this is done, you can play the scene. As you play your scene (please make sure that the **Animator** window is visible), you should be able to start in the **idle** mode (i.e., no keys pressed), and you should be able to modify the value for the parameters **xPos** and **yPos** and see the 3D character successively strafing to the left and to the right or walking forward or back.

Note that this blend tree is only controlled from the **Animator** window for the time being. To be able to control it from your keyboard, we will need to be able to modify the parameters **xPos** and **yPos** from the code, and we will do that in the next section.

CONTROLLING A 2D BLEND TREE FROM A SCRIPT

In the previous section we used two parameters to modify our 2D blend tree; however, we now need to control these parameters from our script. So let's go ahead:

- Please open the script **ControlNPC**.

- Add the following code to the **Update** function (new code in bold).

```
float xPos, yPos;

xPos = Input.GetAxis ("Horizontal");

yPos = Input.GetAxis ("Vertical");

anim.SetFloat ("xPos", xPos);

anim.SetFloat ("yPos", yPos);

speed = yPos;


//control.SimpleMove (transform.forward * speed);

control.SimpleMove (transform.forward * yPos + transform.right *
xPos);
```

In the previous code:

- We declare the variables **xPos** and **yPos** that will be used to map the keys pressed to the parameters on the **Animator Controller**.

- We then capture whether the left and right arrow keys were pressed using the **Horizontal** axis.

- We also capture whether the up and down arrow keys were pressed using the **Vertical** axis.

- We set the parameters **xPos** and **yPos** from the **Animator Controller** accordingly.

- Finally, we set the translating speed with the value of **yPos**.

You can now save your code. As you play the scene, you should see that by pressing he arrow keys you can control the strafing movement as well as the ability for the 3D character to move forward and back.

The only issue is that when you are strafing to the right of left, while the corresponding animation is played properly, the character doesn't actually move to the left or to the right. We will solve this by using the following code (new code in bold) in the **Update** function.

```
//control.SimpleMove (transform.forward * speed);
control.SimpleMove (transform.forward * yPos + transform.right *
xPos);
```

In the previous code:

- We comment the previous line.

- We then use the same function to move the character, but this time, we account for the left and right arrow keys by combining the variable **xPos** to the function **transform.right**.

- In other words, if the right arrow is pressed (i.e., **xPos = 1**) we will move the character to the right, and if the left arrow is pressed (i.e., **xPos = -1**) we will move the character to the left.

You can now save your code, and test the scene; you should see that when you press the right arrow, the character actually moves to the right.

LEVEL ROUNDUP

In this chapter, we have learned more about creating and using a 2D blend tree and how to blend between animations using two parameters this time. So, we have, again, covered some significant ground compared to the last chapter.

Checklist

You can consider moving to the next chapter if you can do the following:

- Create a 2D blend tree.

- Control the blend tree from your script.

- Create new motions for your blend tree.

- Play an animation in reverse for a specific motion.

Quiz

Now, let's check your knowledge! Please answer the following questions or specify if these statements are either correct or incorrect. The solutions are on the next page.

1. A 2D blend tree uses two parameters.

2. The parameters used for a 2D blend tree can be mapped onto a plane.

3. The method **Input.GetAxis** returns values that range between -1 and 1.

4. It is possible to play an animation in reverse using a blend tree.

5. A 2D blend tree can only be using Boolean parameters.

6. The function **SetFloat** can be used to set the value of a float parameter.

7. The function **SetFloatValue** can be used to set the value of a float parameter.

8. A blend tree can be created after right-clicking on the canvas.

9. The method **SimpleMove** can be used to move a character along the x and y axes.

10. By default, an animator controller includes one layer.

Quiz Solutions

Now, let's check if you have answered the questions correctly.

1. True.

2. True.

3. True.

4. True.

5. False.

6. True.

7. False.

8. True.

9. True.

10. True.

Challenge 1

Now that you have managed to complete this chapter and that you know how to use several C# methods in Unity, you could try to create other animations and combine them within a 2D blend tree.

5

POLISHING-UP THE CHARACTER AND ADDING ANIMATIONS

In this section, we will start to include more animations and we will also look at features that make it possible to re-use animations (and states) for several characters.

After completing this chapter, you will be able to:

- Fix any issue related to textures for imported characters.

- Create and apply jumping animations (with gravity) to characters.

- Apply the same **Animator Controller** to two different characters.

The code solutions for this chapter are in the **resource pack** that you can download by following the instructions included in the section entitled "Support and Resources for this Book".

ADDING THE JUMPING MOVEMENT

While in the previous section we have created 1D and 2D blend trees, in this section we will create a jumping animation that will be linked to one of these trees so that we can trigger a jumping movement while the character is walking.

If you would prefer not to use Mixamo, the animations used in this chapter are available in your resource pack that you can download by following the instructions included in the section entitled "**Support and Resources for this Book**".

The first thing is to create the jumping movement:

- Please open Mixamo: **http://wwww.mixamo.com**.

- Look for animation with the words "big jump" in the search window.

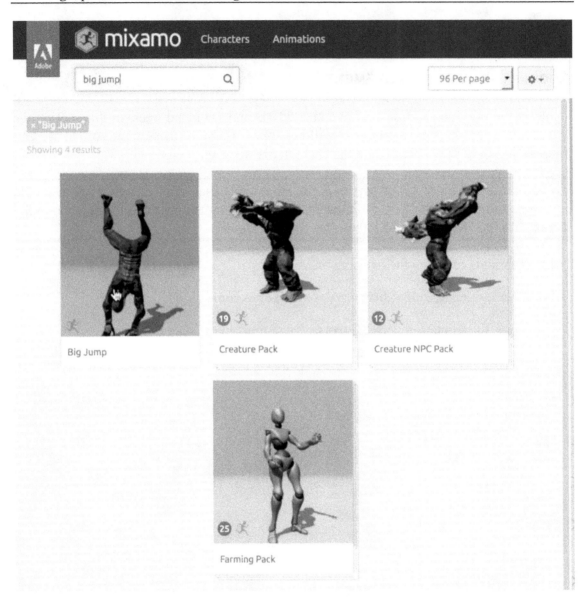

Figure 5-1: Looking for a jumping animation

- Select the first animation in the result lists called **Big Jump** and apply it to your character as we have done previously.

Figure 5-2: Applying the new animation

You should then see, as in the previous figure, that your character, in the right-hand side of the screen, is jumping.

So it's now time to download this animation.

- Please click on the button labelled **Download**.

- Save it to your hard drive using the format **FBX for Unity (FBX)**.

- It should save as **dreyar_m_aure@Big Jump.fbx**.

Once this is done, please import the file that you have just created by dragging and dropping the animation to the **Project** folder in Unity.

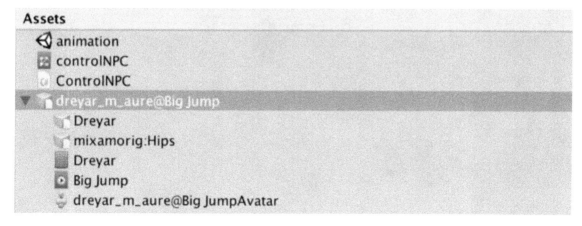

Figure 5-3: Importing the animation

- Click on this asset.

- Using the **Animator** window, then click on the tab called **Model**, change the scale factor to **0.1**, and press the **Apply** button.

What we'd like now is for the character to jump when we press the space bar, so we will initially control the jumping movement using the **Animator** window through a dedicated parameter (a trigger), and then control this trigger through our script.

- Please create a new state call **jump**, linked to an animation called **Big Jump**. The idea is that we should be able to transition from any state in the blend tree to the jumping movement and then back to the blend tree again. To do so, we will create a **Trigger** parameter called **startJump**.

- Please create a new **Trigger** parameter called **startJump**.

- Create a transition from the 2D blend tree to the state called **jump** with the trigger **startJump** as a condition for the transition to occur.

- Create a transition from the state called **jump** to the 2D blend tree with no specific condition yet, so that the **Animator Controller** transitions back to the blend tree once the jump is complete.

You can now play the scene and check that if you set the trigger called **startJump** that the character actually jumps.

One of the issue that you may spot is that the character is **moving** back to its original position after the jump, and we will fix this issue in the next section.

CONTROLLING THE JUMPING MOVEMENT

In the previous section we were able to trigger the **jumping** movement through the **Animator** window; however, the character was going back to its initial position; so we will address this issue now.

- In the **Animator** window, please select the state called **jump**.

- In the **Animator** window, select the tab called **Animations** and select (i.e., tick) the options called **Loop Time** and **Loop Pose**.

So at this stage the character should be able to jump on the spot; however, to make it go forward, we will use some C# code:

- Please open the script called **ControlNPC**.

- Add the following code to it (new code in bold).

```
if (info.IsName ("walking"))

    print ("We are in the walking mode");


if (info.IsName ("jump")) control.SimpleMove (transform.forward *
1.5f);


if (Input.GetKeyDown (KeyCode.Space)) anim.SetTrigger
("startJump");
```

In the previous code:

- We check that we are in the state called **jump**.

- And if this is the case, we move the character forward at the speed of **1.5 meters per second**.

- We then check that the **SPACE** key is pressed, and set the trigger **startJump** accordingly if this is the case.

After saving your code, you can play the scene, click on the **Game** view, and check that after pressing the space bar that the character jumps forward, as per the next figure.

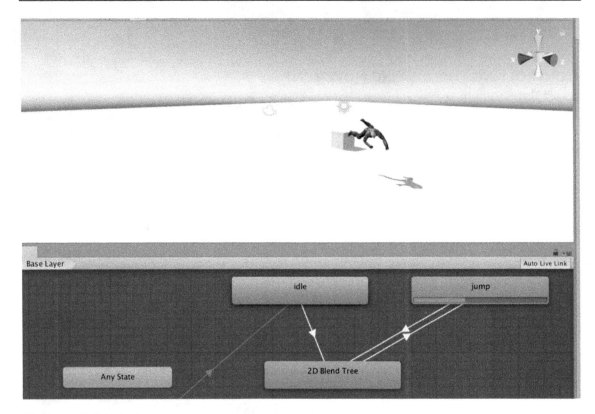

Figure 5-4: Polishing the jumping movement

So you can see that in this case, the animation is more realistic in the sense that the character jumps forward without going back to its original position.

USING THE SAME ANIMATOR CONTROLLER FOR DIFFERENT CHARACTERS

In the previous section, we managed to combine a jumping movement and a blend tree. In this section we will use the same **Animator Controller** for two characters. The transitions and trees will be the same; however, the animations will be different.

If you would prefer not to use Mixamo, the animations used in this section are available in the resource pack that you can download by following the instructions included in the section entitled "**Support and Resources for this Book**".

The first things we need to do is to create a new character along with its corresponding animations for walking, running, strafing, or jumping; for this purpose, you can do the following:

- Open the Mixamo page in your browser.

- Click on the tab called **Characters**.

- I have chosen the character called **Douglas** but you can choose any other character if you wish.

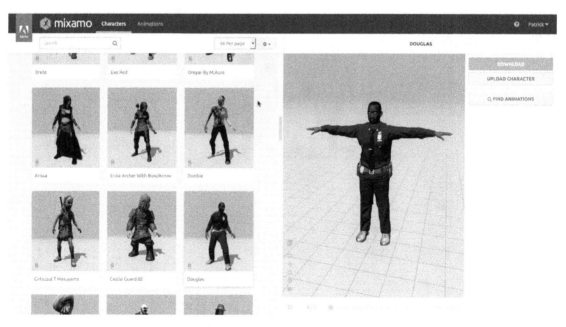

Figure 5-5: Selecting the character called Douglas

- Click on the tab labelled **Animations**.

- Look for the same animations that you have used for the previous character (i.e., **Big Jump, Walking, idle, Straf Right, etc**.) and export each of these to your hard drive. These don't have to be the same animations; we just need to have an animation for the different states that we created for the character **Dreyar** initially.

- Please select the animation and export it as we have done previously.

- Repeat this step for all the necessary animations.

Once you have created the different animations for your new character, we will manage to re-use all the Finite State Machines initially employed for the character called **Dreyar** and to apply them to the second character, called Douglas, so that we don't have to recreate them. This will save you a lot of time:

- Please import the **Douglas** files that you have downloaded from Mixamo to Unity. You may create a new folder for this purpose.

- Drag and drop the asset **Douglas@Idle** from the **Project** window to the **Scene**.

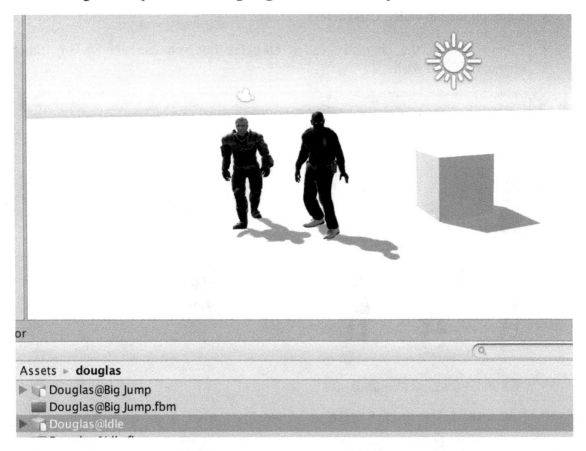

Figure 5-6: Adding the character Douglas

- This will create a new object called **Douglas@Idle**, and you can rename it if you wish.

Once all these files have been imported, we will need to identify the corresponding animations and amend their name so that we can tell between the animations for the characters **Douglas** and **Dreyar**.

Let's start with the Big-Jump animation.

- Please select the asset "**Douglas@Big Jump**" in the **Project** window.

Assets ▸ **douglas**
▶ 📄 Douglas@Big Jump
📁 Douglas@Big Jump.fbm

Figure 5-7: Modifying the jumping animation for Douglas

- In the **Inspector**, modify the name of the animation to **Douglas - Big Jump**.

Douglas – Big Jump

Figure 5-8: Modifying the name of jumping animation for Douglas

- Also tick the **Loop Time** and **Loop Pause** attributes.

Loop Time ✓
Loop Pose ✓

Figure 5-9: Looping the animation

- Apply these changes by clicking on the button labelled **Apply**.

Revert   Apply

Figure 5-10: Applying changes

- Perform the same actions for all the other animations imported for Douglas so that the name of the animations includes the word **Douglas**.

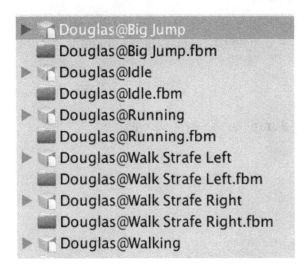

Figure 5-11: Changing the name of the animations

Once this is done:

- Add a **Character controller** to **Douglas** and change its **center y** attribute to **1**, as per the next figure.

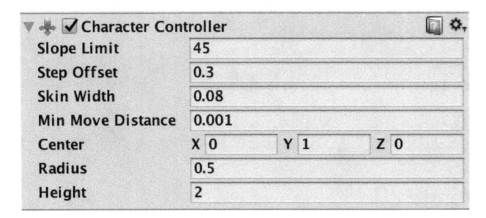

Figure 5-12: Modifying the Character Controller

- Finally, please add the script **ControlNPC** to the object **Douglas**, so that it can be controlled.

At this stage we just need to create a new Animator Controller for Douglas; for this purpose, we will create a new type of Animator Controller called **Animator Override Controller**; this type of controller makes it possible to reuse an **Animator Controller** but to apply different animations to it. In our case we want to reuse the **Animator Controller** employed for **Dreyar** and apply animations created for **Douglas**. So let's go ahead;

- Create a new **Animator Override Controller**: from the **Project** window, select **Create | Animator Override Controller**.

- Select this new controller, and using the **Inspector,** select the correct animations for each of the fields present in the column labelled **Override** (i.e., click on the corresponding cogwheel to the right of each field), as per the next figure:

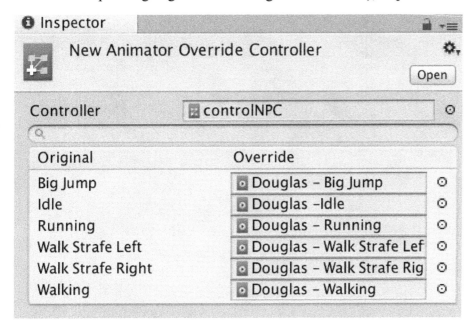

Figure 5-13: Adding animations

Once this is done:

- Please select the object called **Douglas** present in the scene (e.g., using the **Hierarchy** window).

- Using the **Inspector**, drag and drop the **Animator Override Controller** that you have just created to the field called **Controller** for the component **Animator**, as per the next figure.

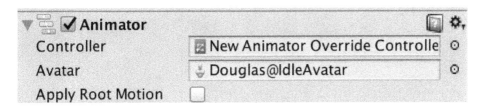

Figure 5-14: Applying the new controller

[129]

That's it; you can now play your scene and you should be able to control both characters simultaneously.

FIXING THE TEXTURES FOR THE CHARACTER

In some cases, it may be that when you import the character that you have created in Mixamo, that its textures do not appear properly in Unity. Thankfully, this can be fixed easily, and we will see how in this section.

- Please select the asset **dreyar_aure@Idle** from the **Project** window (or the 3D character that you have imported in Unity).

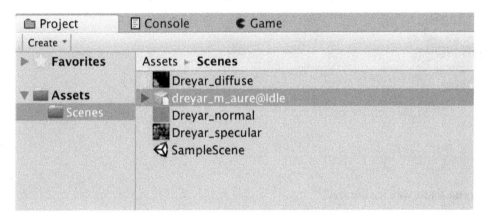

Figure 5-15: Selecting the Idle character

- In the **Inspector** window, select the tab called **Materials**.

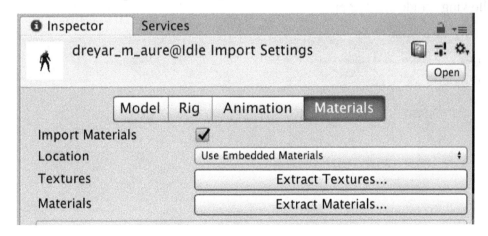

Figure 5-16: Extracting textures

- Then click on the button labelled **Extract Textures...**

- Unity will then ask you to specify the folder where the textures are stored; by default, it will select the folder where the asset (the model) has been imported, so you can just click on the button labelled **Choose**.

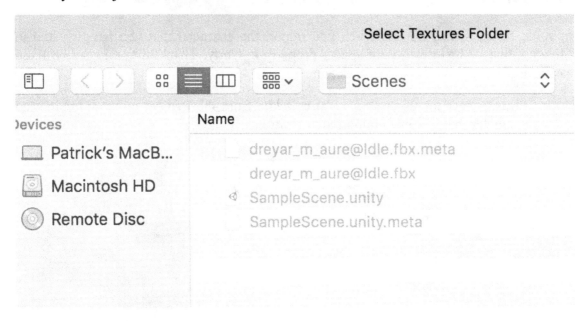

Figure 5-17: Selecting the folder with the textures

- After a few seconds, Unity will find and apply the necessary texture(s) to your character.

- The following window may appear.

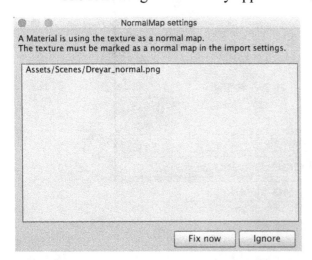

Figure 5-18: Fixing normals

- Please click the button labelled "**Fix Now**"; you should now see that your character is textured properly.

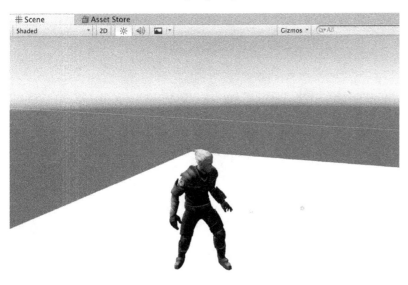

Figure 5-19: The character with proper textures applied

This should fix the issue with any other animated versions of the character Dreyar.

LEVEL ROUNDUP

Summary

In this chapter, we have managed to look further into animations, by using the same Animator Controller for two different characters, and by creating and controlling the jumping movement of our characters. So well done! This is quite a significant leap from the last chapter.

Quiz

Now, let's check your knowledge! Please answer the following questions (the answers are included in the resource pack) or specify whether they are correct or incorrect.

1. The method **IsName** makes it possible to know the active state for a specific **Animator Controller**.

2. In Unity it is possible to re-use the same **Animator Controller** for different characters.

3. It is possible to modify the center of a **Character Controller**.

4. An **Animator Override Controller** can be used to re-use an **Animator Controller** but with different animations.

5. It is possible to change the looping features of an animation imported in Unity as part of an FBX character.

6. It is possible to scale-up or down an FBX character that has been imported in Unity.

7. The tab called Materials, for an imported animated character, can be used to solve issues related to the textures of this character.

8. The method called **SimpleMove** can be employed to move a **Character Controller**.

9. The method **SetTrigger** can be used to change the value of a **Trigger** parameter that belongs to an **Animator Controller**.

10. The method **GetTheKeyDown** can be used to detect the key that has been pressed.

Quiz Solution

Now, let's check your knowledge!

1. True.

2. True.

3. True.

4. True.

5. True.

6. True.

7. True.

8. True.

9. True.

10. False (it is the method **GetKeyDown**).

6
FREQUENTLY ASKED QUESTIONS

This chapter provides answers to the most frequently asked questions about the features that we have covered in this book. Please also note that some **videos are also available on the companion** site (http://learntocreategames.com/book-videos/) to help you with some of the concepts covered in this book.

IMPORTING ASSETS

How do I import an animated Character?

Drag and drop your 3D character to the **Project** view in Unity.

How can I fix textures when they don't appear on the character that I just imported?

- Please select the 3D character from the **Project** window.

- In the **Inspector** window, select the tab called **Materials**.

- Click on the button labelled **Extract Textures**.

- Unity will then ask you to specify the folder where the textures are stored; by default, it will select the folder where the asset (the model) has been imported, so you can just click on the button labelled **Choose**.

How can I create animated characters?

Many software can be used to animate your characters such as Blender, Fuse or Maya. This being said, these may require a steep learning curve, and you may for the time being use pre-rigged characters to use them in Unity until you feel comfortable with and proficient in 3D model creation.

What is the best format to import 3D characters in Unity?

FBX is the preferred format for 3D characters to be used in Unity.

CONTROLLING CHARACTERS

What is a Finite State Machine?

The idea behind a finite state machine is that that the software, or the game for our purpose, will include several states, but will be in one state and one state only at any given time. In terms of 3D animation, this means that we can define several possible states for a 3D character, and that throughout the lifespan of the game, the character will be in one of these states.

What is an Animator Controller?

In Unity an Animator Controller makes it possible to control the different states for a 3D character, the corresponding animation and transition also. Using an Animator Controller, you can make your character more believable in terms of 3D animation and behavior, as the characters will transition to different states based on parameters influenced by the environment (e.g., presence of objects ahead or proximity to a target) or the internal state of the NPC (e.g., health, ammunition, etc.).

What is a transition?

In Unity, it is possible, through the use of Animator Controllers to create transitions between states, sometimes based on conditions. These conditions can be based on the value of some parameters. By combining these parameters, you can create relatively simple or complex conditions for a transition to occur. For example, you could state that the NPC will transition from the state IDLE to the state FOLLOW_PLAYER if it can see the player and if the player is within four meters.

Is it possible to control an Animator Controller through a Script?

Yes, using a C# script, you can define the current state for a specific **Animator Controller**, and also trigger transitions by modifying the value of associated parameters.

USING BLEND TREES

What is a blend-tree?

In Unity, a blend tree makes it possible to smoothly blend between animations based on one or more parameters; for example, the animation for a character could be blended from a walking to a running animation based on its speed.

Is it possible to control an Animator Controller through a Script?

Yes, since the blending is based on one or several parameters; by modifying the value of these parameters from a C# script, you can then effectively modify the blend tree and trigger blending between states.

What is an Animator Override?

This type of controller makes it possible to reuse an animator controller but to apply different animations to it. So for example, you could have two NPCs using the same Animator Controller but with different animations for each state; this would be made possible through the use of an **Animator Override**.

7
THANK YOU

I would like to thank you for completing this book. I trust that you feel proficient in 3D Animation and Unity. This book is the first in the series "Getting Started" that covers particular aspects of Unity, so it may be time to move on to the next books where you will get started with even more specific features. You can find a description of these forthcoming books on the official page http://www.learntocreategames.com/books/.

In case you have not seen it yet, you can subscribe to the Facebook group using the following link. It includes a community of like-minded game developers who share ideas and are ready to help you with your game projects.

http://facebook.com/groups/learntocreategames/

You may also subscribe to the mailing list to receive weekly updates and information on how to create games and improve your skills.

http://learntocreategames.com/subscribe/

So that the book can be constantly improved, I would really appreciate your feedback. So, please leave me a helpful review on Amazon letting me know what you thought of the book and also send me an email (learntocreategames@gmail.com) with any suggestions you may have. I read and reply to every email.

Thanks so much!!

www.ingramcontent.com/pod-product-compliance
Lightning Source LLC
Chambersburg PA
CBHW080535060326
40690CB00022B/5135